More Devotions
from Everyday Things

Enjoy the Adventure!
Sammy Chandler
Proverbs 16:9
:)

More Devotions from Everyday Things

by

Tammy Chandler

WordCrafts

More Devotions from Everyday Things
Copyright © 2014
Tammy Chandler

Cover photography & design by David Warren

Scriptures marked NIV are taken from THE HOLY BIBLE, NEW INTERNATIONAL VERSION®, NIV® Copyright © 1973, 1978, 1984, 2011 by Biblica, Inc.® Used by permission. All rights reserved worldwide.

Scripture quotations marked HCSB are taken from the Holman Christian Standard Bible®, Copyright © 1999, 2000, 2002, 2003, 2009 by Holman Bible Publishers. Used by permission. Holman Christian Standard Bible®, Holman CSB®, and HCSB® are federally registered trademarks of Holman Bible Publishers.

Scripture quotations marked (ESV) are from The Holy Bible, English Standard Version®(ESV®), copyright © 2001 by Crossway, a publishing ministry of Good News Publishers. Used by permission. All rights reserved.

Scripture quotations marked NKJV are taken from the New King James Version®. Copyright © 1982 by Thomas Nelson, Inc. Used by permission. All rights reserved.

Scripture quotations marked KJV are taken from the Authorized Version, commonly referred to as the King James Version; public domain.

Scripture marked NAS are taken from the NEW AMERICAN STANDARD BIBLE®, Copyright © 1960, 1962, 1963, 1968, 1971, 1972, 1973, 1975, 1977, 1995 by The Lockman Foundation. Used by permission.

All rights reserved. No part of this book may be reproduced, stored in a retrieval system, or transmitted in any form or by any means – electronic, mechanical, photocopy, recording, or otherwise – without the prior written permission of the publisher. The only exception is brief quotations for review purposes.

Published by WordCrafts Press
Tullahoma, TN 37388
www.wordcrafts.net

For my family,
who continues to encourage me
to tell my story

Contents

Preface 1
Acknowledgements 3
The Sunflowers 5
Heart-Shaped Puddles 7
The Gnat 9
The Puppy's Birthday 11
The Flip Flops 13
The Fairy Tale 15
The Chair 17
The Pregnant Pony 19
The Altar 21
The Garden Scarecrow 23
The Rearview Mirror 25
Wet Leaves 27
The Bat 29
The Broken Ornament 31
The Coffee Stain 33
The Computer Crash 35
Burnt Marshmallows 37
The Dugout 39

The Broken Eagle 41
The Dress 43
The Personal Trainer 45
Feathers 47
The Red Card 49
The Helmet 51
The Veteran 53
The Roadblock 55
Laser Tag 57
The Bee Sting 59
The Huddle 61
The Tight-Rope Walker 63
The Faucet 65
The Scar 67
Noisy Dogs 69
The Filling 71
The Hole 73
The Catcher's Glove 75
The Pop-up Camper 77
The Island 79
The Lease 81
The Berry Bush 83
The Hidden Painting 85

The Leash	87
The Energy Drink	89
The Olympics	91
The Tongue Depressor	93
Boot Camp for Horses	95
The Timing Belt	97
Witch's Thistle	99
The Orphan	101
The Young Wren	103
The House Fly	106
The Dirty Jerseys	108
Falling Leaves	110
Father's House	112
The Remodeling Project	114
The Tail Wag	116
238,000 Miles	118
The Sewing Machine	120
The New Car	122
The Adventure Continues	124

Preface

More **Devotions from Everyday Things** is a continuation of the journey started in **Devotions from Everyday Things**. Both are devotional books in which you will find spiritual truths illustrated in ordinary things. An uncomplicated approach toward helping you on your journey to finding deeper spiritual truths as you notice how God is at work in the world around you.

How to use this book: The devotions are simple, straightforward, quiet times with God. Each one contains a daily Scripture passage, an illustration connected with an everyday object, a Thought-provoker, and a prayer starter. The Scripture passage allows you to see where the connection to God's Word is; the illustration will help you to apply the principles of Scripture to something you can take with you throughout the day. The Thought-provoker is an opportunity to adjust your thoughts or actions to the principles learned from the devotion; it is also a Journal prompt if you prefer to write your thoughts. The prayer is a conversation starter about the topic of the devotion. It is an opportunity for you to thank Him for what you are learning, and to ask Him for the strength you need to apply new Biblical principles to your thoughts and actions. It is also a time for you to share your burdens and pour out your heart about personal struggles you are facing.

You can also join me at my blog site: www.simplydevotions.wordpress.com. You will find encouragement, updates, and more postings to help keep us all going in this adventure into deeper spiritual truths. It's time to be excited about being a Christian—it's a faith adventure in everyday things.

Thank you for joining me for this adventure in **More Devotions from Everyday Things**. I am so excited you have chosen this book, and I am praying for you to know God in a deeper, richer way because you have chosen this faith adventure. Let's get started.

Acknowledgements

Thank you to my family: John, Jonathan, Jordan and Charity, for their love, prayers and encouragement as we took on the adventure of publishing a second book. Thank you for allowing me to use bits and pieces of our lives together to share our story. Thank you to our parents: Nick and Dore, Jerry and Ginny, and Jim and Esther. You have been great support, and I am so blessed to have you all in our lives. For our brothers and sisters, family members and friends who have encouraged me all along this adventure—thank you.

To our Lighthouse Family—I am so thankful for all of you who pray, support, encourage, recommend and stand with me every step of the way. Kim, Jennifer, Melissa and Tammy - thank you for reading, inputting and praying this book into existence—such good friends. Thanks.

To the WordCrafts Press team—you are wonderful, and I am so thankful God saw fit for us to meet in a coffee shop. Carpe Café—thanks for giving us a place to meet, talk and be able to learn from each other.

Finally, thank you, reader, for choosing to join us on this great adventure in life. Seeing God at work in the everyday things around us is a choice, and a blessing, and I am so thankful you are a part of it.

To God be the glory, great things HE has done!

Tammy Chandler

More Devotions from Everyday Things

The Sunflowers

Praise the Lord, O my soul; all my inmost being, praise his holy name. Praise the Lord, O my soul, and forget not all his benefits - who forgives all your sins and heals all your diseases, who redeems your life from the pit and crowns you with love and compassion, who satisfies your desires with good things so that your youth is renewed like the eagle's. The Lord works righteousness and justice for all the oppressed.

Psalm 103:1-6, NIV

My daughter decided to plant sunflowers in our garden. Friends of ours had sunflowers that stood tall and straight—towering over their garden of beautiful vegetables and plants. The sunflowers gave the birds all the food they wanted, and helped protect the growing veggies from being assaulted as they grew. We thought the sunflowers would help our garden the same way, so our friends shared some seeds with us and we planted a row of them. And, yes, did they grow. They grew three feet, then four, then five until they stood six feet tall, with large yellow heads and strong, green stems. The sunflowers soon stood guard over our garden. I watched them. I was fascinated by their presence. Early in the mornings, their heads would droop toward the ground, but as the sun came up, they lifted their heads up and followed the sun's rays all day; every day. Only at night did their heads droop again, as if resting, getting ready for tomorrow's adventure of following the sun.

Our faces should lift to the Son—Jesus. Each morning, we should shed our sleepiness, and even our thoughts of hopelessness or despair, and our faces should follow the Son. Each day, we should find joy in knowing we have a Son to follow—the One who is guiding our way. We should see our spiritual journey as an adventure—a daily opportunity to reach for the sky and catch the rays of pleasantness that shine down from our Redeemer's loving face. Each day, we should be grateful that we follow the Son—to know Him in such a personal and intimate way, and not to forget all His benefits and blessings toward us. Each night, we can lay our heads on our pillows, knowing that tomorrow will be another adventure into His grace and goodness.

Thought provoker: Does your face lift to the Son—your Redeemer—each morning? Do you follow His loving direction throughout the day? Do you see your spiritual journey as an adventure? Take some time to think about what the Son is asking of you and then decide to lift your face to His direction and follow it—one day at a time.

Lord, thank You for the sunflowers that lift their heads to the sun. Help me to lift my head to You, the Son of God, and to know that You will fill my life with good things as I move forward in Your love. Help me to be a Son-follower today. Amen.

Notes/Insights:

More Devotions from Everyday Things

Heart-Shaped Puddles

❦

For the word of the LORD is right, and all His work is trustworthy. He loves righteousness and justice; the earth is full of the LORD's unfailing love. The heavens were made by the word of the LORD, and all the stars, by the breath of His mouth. He gathers the waters of the sea into a heap; He puts the depths into storehouses. Let the whole earth tremble before the LORD; let all the inhabitants of the world stand in awe of Him.

Psalm 33:4-8, HCSB

Ava and I were out for a walk. It had been a particularly difficult week for our family. Emotional decisions were made, friends had suffered the tragic loss of a pet, and the rain had been relentless. Finally, a break in the weather meant Ava and I could head outdoors for our morning walk.

As we walked, I noticed my mood start to change. Whispered prayers to comfort our friends and to lift our children's spirits began to help my own heart to seek hope. Ava and I dodged puddles as we moved down the block, and as I looked ahead down the road, I noticed them. Heart-shaped rain puddles. There were three of them in a row. I smiled as I thought, "How like you, Father, to send three little reminders on the path I am walking at this moment to remind me that I am truly loved, truly treasured and remembered, even during this time of emotional weariness." God placed three puddles, three heart-shaped puddles, in my path to remind me of His faithful love for me and my family. I turned my attention from my thoughts, and listened. I heard the birds in the trees and felt the gentle breeze. I saw flowers opening new blossoms toward the sky after the rain, and I saw rays of sunshine peeking through the clouds.

So many times God's love is right under our noses, or right in the midst of difficult circumstances, and when we take time to notice, it lifts our spirits and gives us hope. I would have missed the heart-shaped puddles if I had not taken a moment to look up, look ahead and see what God had put in my path. And, if I had missed the puddles, I probably would not have noticed the other blessings around me in nature. Spiritually, we need to be on the lookout for unexpected reminders of His faithful love to us, and let them bring a smile to our souls in spite of the circumstances around us. Let one blessing lead to another, and thank Him for each one—even heart-shaped puddles.

Thought-provoker: Are you in need of a moment to stop and take in all the wonderful reminders of God's faithful love? Take the time—your soul needs it.

Lord, thank You for Your unfailing love. Thank You for the reminders You send us daily to see Your love and hope in the midst of any circumstances. You are so good. Amen.

Notes/Insights:

More Devotions from Everyday Things

The Gnat

~~~

Now as they went on their way, Jesus entered a village. And a woman named Martha welcomed him into her house. And she had a sister called Mary, who sat at the Lord's feet and listened to his teaching. But Martha was distracted with much serving. And she went up to him and said, "Lord, do you not care that my sister has left me to serve alone? Tell her then to help me." But the Lord answered her, "Martha, Martha, you are anxious and troubled about many things, but one thing is necessary. Mary has chosen the good portion, which will not be taken away from her."

Luke 10:38-42, ESV

Have you ever noticed when you try to focus on something—I mean really focus and pay close attention—something happens? For me, it was a gnat. I should have been giving my undivided attention to my studies, but I could not focus. There was a gnat buzzing around my head, then diving at the light I was using, then disappearing for a moment, then buzzing around my nose—on and on it went. I tried to squish him, but he was too quick for me. I tried moving, but he followed me. He kept buzzing and buzzing and buzzing, until he finally landed on the tabletop.

The busyness of the earthly things around us can be like that gnat. In their own space and proper place, they do not distract us, but when we get focused on something with spiritual implications, all of a sudden they start buzzing around in our minds, distracting us from what is truly important.

Martha had a gnat. And it was a good gnat—serving others. It probably worked well for her when she kept things in context. But, in this case, this gnat distracted her to the point that she lashed out at Jesus—"Do you not care that my sister has left me to serve alone?" I can hear the inflection in her voice, words like "care" "left me" and "serve alone" all getting emphasis. Maybe you have a gnat: time management; ministering; organizing; socializing. They are good things, but they are distractions if not kept in the right context.

Jesus cuts right to the chase and lands the gnat on the tabletop. "Martha, you are anxious and troubled about many things..." Jesus understands the urgent things—the many things that need to get done, but He also understands the important: "...but one thing is necessary." The good portion of spending time at His feet cannot be left unattended, no matter how many urgent gnats seem to be flying around as we rise for the day. We need to land those pesky gnats on the tabletop and tell them they must wait until we have taken time for the one necessary thing—time with Jesus.

Thought-provoker: Do you have urgent gnats that are distracting you from the one necessary thing? Write them down and then tell them they must wait.

Lord, thank You that You call us to spend time at Your feet. Help us to not replace the important with the urgent. Amen.

Notes/Insights:

More Devotions from Everyday Things

The Puppy's Birthday

༄༅

But I, brothers, could not address you as spiritual people, but as people of the flesh, as infants in Christ. I fed you with milk, not solid food, for you were not ready for it. And even now you are not yet ready, for you are still of the flesh. For while there is jealousy and strife among you, are you not of the flesh and behaving only in a human way? For when one says, "I follow Paul," and another, "I follow Apollos," are you not being merely human? What then is Apollos? What is Paul? Servants through whom you believed, as the Lord assigned to each. I planted, Apollos watered, but God gave the growth.

1 Corinthians 3:1-6, ESV

Yes, Ava is growing up. She had a birthday in the late summer, and now she is no longer a puppy by age. No more chewing on furniture; no more whining at the table; no more antics when we are trying to put her in her kennel. At least that is the expectation. What we did not plan on was that Ava did not realize that her birthday means maturity. There are days that she still races around the house with her favorite toy in tow and others when she still whines for food at the table. Just because her age changed, does not mean that her maturity has kept up.

And so it is with us as believers. We are supposed to be growing and changing—becoming more like Christ every day. We reach milestones, anniversaries of our spiritual birthdays, or we achieve age as Christians, but our maturity does not always keep up. Paul reminds us in the passage today that mature Christians eat meat—they digest the Word of God on a regular basis and use its essence to fuel their Christian walk. Maturity means letting go of pettiness—jealousies and strife. Guarding one's own territory or possessions with an eye of envy, or being entangled in a bitter rivalry, are both indications that we have not grown enough in our spiritual walk. When we depend on others to lead us and tell us what the expectations are as our only source of growth, we are still drinking milk. Infants, like puppies, need others to tell them what to do, and when to do it. It is time for us to mature, not just age, in our faith. It is time to rise to the expectations of spiritual adulthood and start eating the meat of the Word for our own good.

Thought provoker: Does your spiritual maturity reflect your spiritual age, or do you have some growing to do in the coming days?

Lord, thank You for Your expectation of growth and maturity, not just age, in our spiritual lives. Help us to consume Your Word, to really "chew" on its meaning and apply it to the core of our beings, to create a change everyone can notice in the coming days, because we want to become more like You. Amen.

Notes/Insights:

More Devotions from Everyday Things

The Flip Flops

> Therefore, since we are surrounded by so great a cloud of witnesses, let us also lay aside every weight, and sin which clings so closely, and let us run with endurance the race that is set before us, looking to Jesus, the founder and perfecter of our faith, who for the joy that was set before him endured the cross, despising the shame, and is seated at the right hand of the throne of God.
>
> Hebrews 12:1-2, ESV

Flip flops are not good running shoes. Our daughter loves to wear flip flops, but when we picked up a family match of soccer one afternoon, she found out the hard way they do not hold up well. She got blisters between her toes and bruises on the tops and sides of her feet where she made contact with the leather soccer ball. When she tried to run, the flip flops would "flop" and it made it difficult for her to pick up speed. They were hindering her from enjoying the time we were having as a family. She contemplated going barefoot to make the running easier, but she quickly found out that was also not a good idea. When playing pick-up soccer, it's best to have on sneakers or cleats.

In our spiritual running, we also need to have the right equipment. Sin, like those flip flops, hinders us from running our best races. It "flops" around as we try to make strides in our spiritual journeys, and it weighs us down. We need the type of shoes that will go the distance—endure the race. What type of spiritual shoes do we need? Jesus tells us focus and joy are the shoes that get the job done. Because He was focused on doing the Father's will, He endured the cross. He also knew the joy was coming. No, we don't always enjoy the race, but we always enjoy the finish line. We have to remember that the hills we traverse, the valleys we go through, they are all part of the race that builds our spiritual character and tests our obedience. Those times make us stronger, steadier, as we go through this life, and when we reach the other side of those trials, we are joyful for God's care and His wisdom in bringing those things to our lives to make us better runners. We need to get rid of whatever is holding us back and run the race with the focus and joy that will get us where we need to be.

So, get the right shoes on—focus and joy—and get running the race God has for you to run.

Thought-provoker: Are you wearing the right shoes and running the spiritual race without "flip flops" hindering you? Ask God to show you how to run a better spiritual race.

Lord, thank You for the spiritual race, and for preparing us with the right equipment. Help us to lay aside all the weights that will hinder us and help us to run races that bring You joy, and us too. Amen.

Notes/Insights:

More Devotions from Everyday Things

The Fairy Tale

‿❦‿

This is a faithful saying and worthy of all acceptance, that Christ Jesus came into the world to save sinners, of whom I am chief. However, for this reason I obtained mercy, that in me first Jesus Christ might show all longsuffering, as a pattern to those who are going to believe on Him for everlasting life. Now to the King eternal, immortal, invisible, to God who alone is wise, be honor and glory forever and ever. Amen.

I Timothy 1:15-17, NKJV

I read fairy tales. Dragons, princes, ladies in distress, kings, queen, evil plotters and court jesters are all members of my imagination. I want the handsome prince to win, the evil plotters to be brought to justice, the dragon tamed and the princess saved. I want the story to turn out right, a happy ending with everyone in a good place—except the bad guy, of course, because he deserves to be unhappy.

Life as it should be. We want our lives to be fairy tales, don't we? We want to be rescued from our terrible job, the dragon that breathes down our neck with deadlines and duties. Or, maybe we want to be saved from the evil plotter—the person who deserves to be in a dungeon for all the gossip and strife they cause in relationships. Or, perhaps, we just need a court jester to make us smile with his silliness and bring some happiness in the midst of a terrible tragedy.

I have good news. We do live a fairy tale. Not what you expected, right? We do not see life as it should be, but neither do the characters in a fairy tale when the story starts. Something is wrong at the beginning—a dangerous dragon threatens the kingdom, or the princess is snatched away from the royal family. What makes the story a fairy tale is that a hero rises up with bravery and strength and he makes the story right again.

Jesus Christ is the hero of every life story. "...Jesus Christ came into the world to save sinners..." There is no more of a tragedy than sin invading the story of humanity and separating us from the great King of Kings. The King Himself comes in bravery and strength, and He makes the story right again. He is our true love—the true Hero that saves the soul, not just the day. He is our fairy tale come true. And one day, He will come and finish the story—a happy ending—eternity with Him.

Thought provoker: Are you living a fairy tale? Not denying reality, but knowing that your True Love is the greatest Hero of all time and He makes the story right. Tell someone today about your Prince of Peace.

Lord, thank You for being my true Love and Hero who will set the story right. Thank You that You have already rescued my soul. I worship You today and I praise You for all You have done. Amen.

Notes/Insights:

More Devotions from Everyday Things

The Chair

"Be still, and know that I am God. I will be exalted among the nations, I will be exalted in the earth." The LORD of hosts is with us; the God of Jacob is our fortress.

Psalm 46:10-11, ESV

I keep a camping chair in the trunk of my car. One of the benefits of being a sports mom is that I get to go to practices. While our sons are out on the fields practicing, I get to sit. I plop my chair down on the sidelines, watch and wait. Sometimes, I take my crochet project with me and work on something, but other times, I just sit. I need to be still. I need to relax. I need the sun to warm my body, and I need the Son to warm my soul. I need to reflect on God's blessings in my life and be thankful for healthy children that are so physical and active.

There are times when it is a great challenge to sit still. I am a doer, and a problem-solver. I do not like to believe there are problems that cannot be solved, or that people do not want God to work in their hearts and change their mindsets. I sometimes have a hard time allowing God to work in *my* heart to become who He wants me to be. Yet, those are the times I need to be still the most and allow God to take over. Not that He will change a single circumstance, or answer a single prayer to my liking—He just needs to take over. He needs to be exalted in my thinking, not just among the nations, but in my heart. He needs to be my fortress and not allow me to solve problems my own way.

My chair has become a symbol of those times when I need to be still. I have started looking forward to those times when I need to sit. I am learning to be grateful for the times He asks me to be still. No busy work, no projects; just God and I having a moment. I need to be reminded of the rest of the verse: "The LORD of hosts is with us." He is with me; He is with you, every step of the way. Yes, He is exalted among the nations, but that happens through individuals. In those quiet moments, when we choose to be still in His presence, He reveals His awesomeness to us, proves His faithfulness to us, and shows us He is God. No problems are too big, no person too far, no project too significant. When we are still, we know that He is God. And that is enough.

Thought-provoker: Have you taken time to be still with God? Are there issues that are keeping you from spending quiet time with Him? Tell Him about them and let Him handle them.

Lord, thank You for allowing us the privilege to be still with You. Thank You that You do not demand we stay busy to prove our love for You. Thank You for quiet times to have moments with You—please don't let us miss them. Amen.

Notes/Insights:

More Devotions from Everyday Things

The Pregnant Pony

> For we know that the whole creation has been groaning together in the pains of childbirth until now. And not only the creation, but we ourselves, who have the firstfruits of the Spirit, groan inwardly as we wait eagerly for adoption as sons, the redemption of our bodies. For in this hope we were saved. Now hope that is seen is not hope. For who hopes for what he sees? But if we hope for what we do not see, we wait for it with patience.
>
> Romans 8:22-25, ESV

We have some great excitement and anticipation going on at the farm. After several months of wondering, the veterinarian confirmed that one of our favorite ponies, Mama Sugar, is expecting her first foal this summer. Sugar is a sweet girl, a fast racer and a favorite of the children who come to ride at the farm. She is gentle, but strong, and she helps riders build their confidence with her skills and her temperament.

Now, we watch, and wait. We watch her belly get bigger as the months go by—we watch as the foal inside her wiggles and moves, and we see tell tale signs that Sugar is ready for this process to move along. Every now and then, we catch her looking back at her enlarged girth and it seems as if she is thinking, "Are you ready yet?"

We all know that Mama Sugar is going to go through labor and delivery in just a few short months. We also know, if all goes as planned, it won't be long until we see her beautiful foal standing on his/her own four feet and flicking a small, bushy tail and eyeing a great big, wonderful world. We anticipate his/her arrival.

This is what creation does each day—creation anticipates the return of Christ. We await that day for our adoption into God's family to become complete—to be with Him—and creation cannot wait to be set free from the curse of sin that humanity brought on the world. This is our hope—Jesus saves—and it is the hope for all of creation. Someday, the "labor and delivery" of anticipating and hoping for the return of Christ will be over and we will be standing in glorious array in the heavenly places, and we will bow to the One Who gave us the ultimate freedom—redemption—and creation will celebrate right along with us.

As we on the farm anticipate Mama Sugar's new arrival, we know it won't be long before the arrival of the King of Kings and Lord of Lords happens and sets us all free to worship Him without the burdens of a sinful, fallen world to hold us back. As we wait for a foal, we are reminded it will not be long before we see our great Savior. Are you ready yet?

Thought-provoker: Do you anticipate the return of Christ?

Lord, thank You that You not only gave us the glorious gift of redemption, but You also give us the wonderful gift of anticipation. We cannot wait to see You. In Jesus' name, Amen.

Notes/Insights:

More Devotions from Everyday Things

The Altar

Shadrach, Meshach, and Abednego answered and said to the king, "O Nebuchadnezzar, we have no need to answer you in this matter. If this be so, our God whom we serve is able to deliver us from the burning fiery furnace, and he will deliver us out of your hand, O king. But if not, be it known to you, O king, that we will not serve your gods or worship the golden image that you have set up."

Daniel 3:16-18, ESV

Be careful where you worship. No, I am not talking about which church you attend, or what type of service it is. Although those both are important, (and should be checked against the Holy Scriptures to be sure they are pleasing in His sight), I am referring to the altar of your heart. When you visit with the Lord in the throne room of your heart—who sits there? When you drop to your knees as a sign of submission, who sits above you? The easy, "church" answer is an indignant, "God the Father, of course." or "Jesus Christ—duh." But, what is the true answer? When playing church is stripped away, when you are alone and no one else is around, or when everyone is around and you are standing in the middle of the church congregation—where do you worship? Do you face the altar of convenience? Culture? Society? Security? Status? Success?

So many of us who have grown up in the church are seeking for a deeper, truer relationship with God; we try hard to cast off "the list" of dos and don'ts to find something better. But then, living by faith gets hard, and we settle for "somewhat satisfied." We have to keep pressing on—we have to refuse to worship the idols that are obstacles, even if it means a fiery furnace. Shadrach, Meshach and Abednego were careful where they worshiped. When everyone else around them bowed to an idol, they stood. When criticized and threatened for their decision, they didn't back down. They put their hearts on the line, and God showed up in a big way for them. They were careful where they worshiped in a world of compromise and anti-God culture. Even in their positions of leadership, they remembered who their King was and they worshiped only at His feet. And remember what happened in the fire? Yes, we know Jesus showed up in the flames—but I cannot help but allow my imagination to enjoy this scene just a little. What do you think they did in those flames? Do you think they discussed the politics of their day? Do you think they talked about their positions or their culture? No, I am pretty sure they worshiped. Be careful where you place your allegiance today, and every day. Worship God and God alone, and then be absolutely awed when He not only brings you through the fire, but He shows up in the midst.

Thought-provoker: Who, or what, is sitting on the throne of your heart today? Take time to be honest with God and if He is not on your heart throne, will you remove the idol and put God back in His rightful place?

Lord, thank You that You are Who we worship. Help us be careful to worship as we should. Amen.

Notes/Insights:

More Devotions from Everyday Things

The Garden Scarecrow

◦※◦

But when he saw the multitudes, he was moved with compassion on them, because they fainted, and were scattered abroad, as sheep having no shepherd. Then saith he unto his disciples, The harvest truly is plenteous, but the labourers are few; Pray ye therefore the Lord of the harvest, that he will send forth labourers into his harvest.

Matthew 9:36-38, KJV

There is a large garden close to our home, and in that garden is a large scarecrow. He stands above the rows of beans and corn and sometimes his hat rustles in the wind. Birds will sit on the fence on the edge of the garden and sit and gaze at the vegetables in the field, but they will not venture into the garden as long as the scarecrow is watching them. The scarecrow does not leave his post, and he does his job by standing in the field and keeping the seed-thieves at bay.

That scarecrow is a reminder of what we are supposed to be. First of all, the scarecrow has to be dressed by the farmer. He doesn't get to pick his style or choose his accessories. He doesn't get to decide whether his plaid shirt is blue or red, or if the pants are jeans or khakis. The Master Farmer, Jesus Christ, has clothed us in righteousness (Isaiah 61:10). We stand dressed in the harvest fields of the world in the garments of salvation and righteousness He chose for us when He redeemed us for His own. I am thankful for the clothing He provides; the Farmer knows just the right clothing to make sure the birds will take notice and keep their distance.

Each scarecrow is also "stuffed" by the farmer. Their inward parts are determined by the farmer—whether it be hay, corn husks or artificial stuffing. The Master Farmer also "stuffs" us. He changes our hearts and minds to be like His, by filling us with His love, patience, joy, thoughts and hope (Philippians 2: 5-8; Galatians 5:22-23).

Then, each scarecrow is placed where the farmer needs it. The farmer decides which garden needs a scarecrow, if the garden needs more than one scarecrow, and which crop the scarecrow will protect. The scarecrow is then placed in the spot of the farmer's choosing, and the scarecrow goes to work protecting the crop. The Master Farmer places each of us in the garden of His choosing—whether a small group of children on a Sunday morning, or an evangelist to an entire nation—He decides where we are to stand and protect the seeds as they grow. We stand guard to keep the spiritual birds away who would snatch away the seed of God's Word from the lives of those in the garden God has given us. Let's get busy protecting those fields.

Thought-provoker: Are you allowing the Master Farmer to clothe, stuff, and place you? Are you doing your job protecting the fields around you?

Lord, thank You for placing each of us as a scarecrow in the fields of life to do a good work for You. Amen.

Notes/Insights:

More Devotions from Everyday Things

The Rearview Mirror

❧❦

"Not that I have already attained, or am already perfected; but I press on, that I may lay hold of that for which Christ Jesus has also laid hold of me. Brethren, I do not count myself to have apprehended; but one thing I do, forgetting those things which are behind and reaching forward to those things which are ahead, I press toward the goal for the prize of the upward call of God in Christ Jesus."

Philippians 3:12-14, NKJV

Observing our teenage son learning to drive has been a great experience. He is cautious, responsible and discerning. Not that I have not had moments of nervousness, but he is showing his maturity in learning from the experiences of other drivers, as well as listening to the voice of his father as he teaches him the skills. Yes, his dad is the main teacher; I get to be the cheerleader. As the cheerleader, I get to sit in the backseat and try not to say too much. One of the things I have learned to do is check the rearview mirror. I can do that from my spot in the back. I can see the cars behind us, but I also get to see the things we have already passed—the things that are fleeting away as we move forward. Sometimes, I pick an object and count how many seconds it takes for it to be completely out of view. On winding roads near our house, that can be a matter of seconds, but straight roads will allow them to stay in view a little longer.

Those images in the rearview mirror are much like our accomplishments, and failures. They seem so big, or daunting, in front of us, but they are soon in the past and fading away. We may sometimes wish for them to stay in view, and sometimes we are glad life takes a hard turn and we cannot see them anymore. God wants us to keep our successes, and our failures, in perspective. We are supposed to be "...forgetting those things which are behind and reaching forward to those things which are ahead..." If my son kept trying to capture all of those objects in the rearview mirror, we would never reach our destination. In fact, we could cause all kinds of chaos if we were chasing those things we see in the mirror. So it is with our lives. God allows us to enjoy moments of accomplishment, but then they pass into the rearview of our lives. We can enjoy them, we can even glance back at them once in awhile, but we cannot chase them down. It is the same for our failures. We can glance back and be thankful that they are behind us, but we cannot keep trying to put them in our present. Rearview means just that, it is in our rear view—we are supposed to be going forward. Let's do that today.

Thought-provoker: Is something in your life taking up your attention that should be in the rear view? Spend time asking God to help you have the right perspective, whether it is a success or a failure.

Lord, thank You that life passes by, that failures, and even successes, don't last forever. Today, I make the choice to put the rear view behind and to drive forward with You. Amen.

Notes/Insights:

More Devotions from Everyday Things

Wet Leaves

A brother offended is harder to be won than a strong city: and their contentions are like the bars of a castle. A man's belly shall be satisfied with the fruit of his mouth; and with the increase of his lips shall he be filled. Death and life are in the power of the tongue: and they that love it shall eat the fruit thereof.

Proverbs 18:19-21, KJV

Fall leaves are beautiful—when they are still attached to the trees. They add color and vibrancy to the weather change, and they perk up our spirits as the many different shades of orange, yellow, red and green paint the landscapes. It is even fun for the kid in all of us when those leaves fall to the ground; we grab a rake, make a pile, and jump in the leaves, or we hear them crunch under our feet as we walk along a wooded path.

What is not fun is when those leaves are thrown to the ground by a thunderous storm and the wet, slippery leaves become perils for walking safely to the car or the mailbox. The leaves fill up the gutters and the curbs and they sit, wet and yucky. Instead of adding to the landscape's beauty, they become a distraction and a disappointment. Someone has to come along with a rake and shovel, or some other equipment and the leaves have to be cleaned up, burned up or thrown away.

Tammy Chandler

Words are like leaves. When they are placed correctly and used wisely, they add beauty and vibrancy to lives. Words can add color to others' lives through encouragement, humor, and love. They can build up a landscape of colorful complements and help others to enjoy peace and beauty in their lives.

But, when the storms of gossip blow through, those words become saturated with sarcasm, bitterness, revenge or hurtfulness, and instead of being beautiful additions to the landscapes of our lives, they become a dangerous, hurtful mess that someone has to clean up and throw away. Those leaves, those words, that were once beautiful pictures of uplifting phrases and words of praise, are turned ugly and sour by gossip.

I am thankful that Jesus is willing to clean up the mess made by gossip through the power of His forgiveness, but we should be very careful to be sure we are not the ones stirring up those storms of gossip, or misusing words to stir up strife. If we find someone who has the litter of gossip strewn in their lives, we should help them clean it up. Our words should be beautiful—filled with encouragement and adding beauty to the lives of those who hear them.

Thought-provoker: Are you adding beauty to the landscapes of lives around you with your words, or are you leaving wet leaves in your wake?

Lord, please, please help us to add beauty to the lives around us through our words and not stir up storms of gossip. Help us to refrain from making things worse with the wrong words. Thank You for words of beauty and encouragement. Amen.

Notes/Insights:

More Devotions from Everyday Things

The Bat

༄༅

Remind them of these things, and charge them before God not to quarrel about words, which does no good, but only ruins the hearers. Do your best to present yourself to God as one approved, a worker who has no need to be ashamed, rightly handling the word of truth.

2 Timothy 2:14-15, ESV

It was quite scary. An ordinary evening at the ball park, with a pretty sunset, quickly changed into sirens, flashing lights and an ambulance ride. It was the fifth inning. Both teams were playing hard, and there had been some tension as tough calls were made on some challenging plays. Our catcher had been strong behind the plate. Nothing was getting past him, and his throws were right on target. He hustled all night, gave a good effort, and even caught a few fouls behind the plate.

I didn't know the batter from the opposing team. He stepped into the box, set up and swung—hard. Strike One. He stepped in and set up again. Swing, and another miss. The exertion, and the anger, began to flush his face. The third pitch, he swung, clipped the ball and popped it up. The catcher reacted, flipped his mask off for a better view of the ball, and in a split second, he was crumpled in a pile on the ground, holding his face with both hands and groaning in agony. The batter had swung the bat all the way around after he foul-tipped it, and had hit the catcher just under the eye. The bat, a tool used to hit the ball over the fence, had become an instrument of danger in a moment of anger. The batter had intended to hit the ball far into the outfield to help his team and score some runs, but his anger had pushed him to swing harder than he should have, and he hurt another player.

And so it happens in our lives. We study the Word of God, prepare to use it as a tool to further the kingdom of God, and in a moment of anger, we use it to crush another's spirit. We react in anger or frustration, and we spew verses at others and argue, instead of living by the words we've learned. We injure others in the game of life.

I believe God warns us in Timothy's letter to make sure He approves of the game plan, then we will play life's game without shame, and we will use His Word as a tool, instead of a dangerous instrument that breaks hearts and "ruins the hearers."

The catcher recovered, but there was a bruise and a scar under his eye for a long time. May we be very careful to use the Word of God to build, not bruise.

Thought-provoker: How well are you handling God's Word?

Lord, help us to build others up for Your glory and to not leave bruises on their hearts. Amen.

Notes/Insights:

More Devotions from Everyday Things

The Broken Ornament

"Behold, My Servant whom I have chosen, My Beloved in whom My soul is well pleased. I will put My Spirit upon Him, And He will declare justice to the Gentiles. He will not quarrel nor cry out, Nor will anyone hear His voice in the streets. A bruised reed He will not break, And smoking flax He will not quench, Till He sends forth justice to victory; And in His name Gentiles will trust."

Matthew 12: 18-21, NKJV

Decorating is an ordeal at our house. We have lots of decorations, and I love to pull them out and make the house look like Christmas. Every room gets a Christmas make over as we transform from our everyday décor to red, green, and white. Thankfully, our children don't mind helping, and putting up the Christmas tree is a family activity. We had been working for awhile, pulling the boxes out of the attic, unwrapping the decorations, and putting them on the tree. I pulled out a special box of ornaments to start working on, when I heard a noise that made my heart sink—tinkling glass. That sound that glass makes when it is broken in little pieces inside a box. I rooted through the box and carefully opened the little white box that made the sound again when I touched it. Inside, a glass-blown nativity set was in pieces. In the jostling of cleaning out the attic during the summer, something must have shifted and put too much pressure on the little box; the ornament inside could not withstand the force, and it broke.

I sat for a moment with the broken pieces in my lap, remembering who had given it to me, and cherishing the friendship that the ornament represented. Then, I gingerly picked up the broken glass and threw it in the trash. There was no remedy for the broken ornament, and it was best to throw away the pieces so that no one would be injured on the shards that were left.

I am so glad that our heavenly Father never sees us as broken ornaments beyond repair. I am glad that we are redeemable in His eyes, and that He finds a way to make each of us a story for His glory. There are times when pressure is applied to us in this life, but God will make sure that no pressure is too much. He will not allow circumstances, trials or tribulations to crush us under their force. None of us will wind up in the trash in God's home—we are each an ornament for His pleasure, and He is pleased to keep us and allow us to reflect His light, not just at Christmas time, but every day we live. How precious we are to Him. How loving He is to us.

Thought-provoker: As we think of the busyness of Christmas time—decorating, gift-giving, family time and memories—we need to remember to let God's light shine through our lives and be His glorious ornament no matter where we are. Do you have a Christmas light in your heart all year?

Lord, thank You that we are never beyond Your redemptive power. Help us to shine as lights in this world for You, not just during the Christmas season, but all year long. Amen.

Notes/Insights:

More Devotions from Everyday Things

The Coffee Stain

You, however, are not in the flesh but in the Spirit, if in fact the Spirit of God dwells in you. Anyone who does not have the Spirit of Christ does not belong to him. But if Christ is in you, although the body is dead because of sin, the Spirit is life because of righteousness. If the Spirit of him who raised Jesus from the dead dwells in you, he who raised Christ Jesus from the dead will also give life to your mortal bodies through his Spirit who dwells in you.

Romans 8:9-11, ESV

I had made it through most of the day with a white sweater on. I normally do not wear light colors, but the sweater was a gift from a friend, and I was enjoying the change in my wardrobe—until my afternoon coffee break. I managed to spill my coffee, just a small splash, on the front of the sweater, right by the buttons. I tried my best to blot it out, but the stain was there. For the rest of the day, I apologized for the stain on my sweater. I told people about it, I brought attention to it. I didn't want people to think that I didn't know it was there, and I wanted to apologize for the stain before they could criticize.

Shame is just like that coffee stain. We have things in our past we keep bringing to others' attention; we apologize for those things; we try our best to blot them out, but the stain is still there. Jesus tells us, we believers are no longer in the flesh but in the Spirit. He not only took our sin, He cleansed our stain (I John 1:9). He erased the shame. Our spiritual sweaters are clean and bright, and there is no more embarrassment to tell others about. Our story becomes one of His holiness outshining our inadequacies and past failures. His life in us gives life to our mortal bodies and His Spirit dwells in us—making it impossible for the stain of shame to be recognized any longer. As you move on in this life, allow Jesus to clean the stains that sin and shame have left on your heart and let Him give you a clean new spiritual sweater to wear—one with a perfect shade of grace and mercy to give your wardrobe the boost it needs in this next year, and many, many years to come.

Thought-provoker: What shame-stain is splotching up your spiritual wardrobe and bringing unnecessary attention to your past? Take it to the Lord and ask Him to wash away the stain with the power of His blood, and then walk in the new spiritual clothes He gives you—grace, mercy and His glory. Hope you have a good, Godly day.

Lord, I thank You for the power You have to remove the stain of shame from my life and make my spiritual wardrobe beautiful for Your glory. Help me to hold my head up as Your child, and let others see You in me this day. Amen.

Notes/Insights:

More Devotions from Everyday Things

The Computer Crash

Now on the first day of the week Mary Magdalene went to the tomb early, while it was still dark, and saw that the stone had been taken away from the tomb. Then she ran and came to Simon Peter, and to the other disciple, whom Jesus loved, and said to them, "They have taken away the Lord out of the tomb, and we do not know where they have laid Him. Then the other disciple, who came to the tomb first, went in also; and he saw and believed.

John 20:1&8, NKJV

It was bound to happen. So many hours, so much data; add emails, contacts, calendars and a virus, and there it went. My computer crashed. I don't know all the technical terms for what happened, but all I saw was a locked-up screen, and instruction boxes covering the screen before I could get the computer shut down. I was upset. I was frustrated—why would God allow all my work, my contacts, my writings to be locked up inside a metal box with little hope of their return? What was I going to do? There was no way I could remember all of that information.

As I waited for my wonderful, "techy" husband to rebuild my files, I began to calm down. Three days passed, and then the first glimmer of hope. As I sat watching him opening the first few files, I could not help but think of a resurrection. Did I dare to think the files would be restored and life would go on with the information in tact? What would it be like on the other side of this computer meltdown?

I thought of the disciples. Their hopes and dreams—the knowledge they had of Jesus as the Messiah—was shattered in their hearts as He hung on that cross. They left Calvary upset, frustrated, hurting. They were probably asking, "Why, God? How could this have happened? We left everything to know Him; to follow Him and there is no way we can keep on believing now." And yet, three days later—did they dare to hope? As the women came back from the tomb, declaring crazy ideas of a resurrected Lord, was there a possibility of restoration? Was there truly a life to live on the other side of the sorrow and pain they had just experienced?

Yes—a resounding yes. Because of Jesus, there is hope. There is restoration. There is life after the meltdown—the demise of a marriage; the loss of a loved one; the ravages of an illness. There is a loving God who will not leave you in the darkness of sorrow or the depths of despair. He will restore you. He will help you go on—and life will be sweeter on the other side of restoration.

Thought-provoker: In what areas of your life do you need restoration? Do you have hope?

Lord, You are the great Hope-Giver. Thank you for restoration, and thank You for Your resurrection that shows us Your awesome power. Amen.

Notes/Insights:

More Devotions from Everyday Things

Burnt Marshmallows

~~~

Flee from sexual immorality. Every other sin a person commits is outside the body, but the sexually immoral person sins against his own body. Or do you not know that your body is a temple of the Holy Spirit within you, whom you have from God? You are not your own, for you were bought with a price. So glorify God in your body.

I Corinthians 6:18-20, ESV

I love camping. Our pop-up camper gives the feel of being outdoors, with the benefits of a real mattress and running water. The slower pace, the nature trails, and the beautiful sunsets are all part of the camping experience. But one of the best parts of camping happens after the sun goes down. The wood gets stacked, the kindling is lit, and before long, there is a big, roaring fire. Some long poles, and puffy, white marshmallows, and voila. Dessert by firelight.

Now, some campers think I'm crazy, but I protect my marshmallows. I either roast them a distance from the flame, or I use tinfoil. Yes, tinfoil. I wrap the side of the marshmallow that faces the fire with tinfoil, because I cannot stand the taste of a burnt marshmallow. I love the toasted flavor, but the marshmallow cannot turn black, or worse, catch on fire.

Relationships are the same way. The fire represents passion, or physical intimacy. The marshmallow represents the relationship, and the distance or tinfoil represent healthy boundaries. If the relationship is exposed to too much passion, it is destroyed and devoured—burnt up with the wrong kind of fire. But, when a relationship is protected from passion in the beginning, when the right kinds of boundaries are set for passion, time alone, and physical intimacy, the relationship toasts to perfection—friendship, romance, thoughtfulness, selflessness and sacrifice are allowed to develop in healthy ways that will sustain a great relationship over a lifetime.

You know what else is interesting about that fire? When you wait long enough, the embers sustain heat without flame, so you can stick a marshmallow in close, and it still won't burn. That's marriage. When the relationship is honoring to God, when you follow His plan and commit to one spouse for a lifetime, He allows the passion and physical intimacy to be an integral part of the sustaining heat, but it blesses the relationship instead of devouring it. God is so awesome. Protect your relationships like marshmallows, and enjoy God's perfect recipe for a sweet, lifelong love.

Thought-provoker; Are you too close to passion's fire in a relationship in your life? Get back. Ask God, today, to show you the safe boundaries you need to keep your life from being burned by the wrong kinds of passions, and then be willing to obey Him in this area of your life.

Lord, keep my relationships pleasing and honoring in Your sight. Where I have not been pleasing, I ask Your forgiveness and today, I commit to living in honor of You in all areas of my life. Make my boundaries safe, healthy and whole. Amen.

Notes/Insights:

More Devotions from Everyday Things

The Dugout

And straightway Jesus constrained his disciples to get into a ship, and to go before him unto the other side, while he sent the multitudes away. And when he had sent the multitudes away, he went up into a mountain apart to pray: and when the evening was come, he was there alone. But the ship was now in the midst of the sea, tossed with waves: for the wind was contrary. And in the fourth watch of the night Jesus went unto them, walking on the sea.

Matthew 14:22-25, KJV

Our oldest son plays baseball, and so the fields close to our home have become quite familiar through the years. There's the actual infield—with the bases and the pitcher's mound, and there's the tall fence and backstop that protect the fans from fly balls. There is also a cement dugout, painted dark green, with a long bench and a few shelves for the boys to set their helmets on. This dugout is a place where the boys can retreat when they are coming off the field and waiting their turns at bat. It's a place to rest, get out of the sun on a hot summer's day, grab a drink from the cooler, and get ready to get back into the game. It is also a place to consult with their coach and find out if there is something they need to do differently, or catch a word of encouragement from their team mates. No one criticizes the boys for taking a short breather between innings to get out of the sun, or to sit for a few moments while they wait to bat. Why not? Because they are supposed to take a break in the dugout.

What is not alright is for the boys to stay in the dugout throughout the game. The game is not played in the dugout—it is played on the field. Jesus took time away from the crowds and out of the spotlight, but He did not stay on that mountain alone. He did not pull out of ministry and decide to go off on His own. He did take time to be alone with the Father, but He returned to ministering to His disciples—He even came in the midst of a storm.

And so it is for us in the game of life. It is totally acceptable to take a break—to go spend time with our heavenly Coach for some encouragement, or grab a spiritual drink of refreshment so we can return to the game and work toward victory. Yes, there are times when the game is very tough, but He asks us to join Him back on the field and keep playing for His team. We follow His example, and we get back in the game.

Thought-provoker: Are you spending too much time in the dugout and not enough time in the field?

Lord, thank You for rest and refreshment, but help us to remember You gave us those things so we could get back in the game and be strong players for Your glory. Amen.

Notes/Insights:

More Devotions from Everyday Things

The Broken Eagle

"Comfort, comfort My people," says your God. But those who trust in the LORD will renew their strength; they will soar on wings like eagles; they will run and not grow weary; they will walk and not faint.

Isaiah 40:1 & 31, HCSB

We visited a rehabilitation ground for wounded birds in the mountains. There were beautiful birds—hawks, owls, cranes, and eagles. The American Bald Eagle sat alone on his perch. His piercing eyes were calm and focused. He did not need a chain on his leg or a cover over his cage. He could not fly. A hunter had shot him through the wing with an arrow, but the eagle refused to die. He flew away, and a compassionate hunter had found the bird and turned him in to the rehabilitation center.

The caretakers explained the wounds each bird had sustained in the wild; arrows, bullets, fishing line, sometimes just plain cruel, inhumane tortures. Each bird was rescued, and now it had a home in the shelter of the rehabilitation center. They were safe, but they were wounded. There were some, through the expertise of the veterinarians and trainers, who were able to return to the wild. They carried scars, but they were able to fly freely again. Pictures of these birds, along with smiling team members, were posted on a brightly colored wall with names and departure dates. It was the celebration wall for those who were able to return to their lives and habitats.

I kept thinking about that eagle. He was meant to be free and soar among the clouds, but he was perched, unable to even leave the sanctuary on his own. How many times has the enemy wounded a saint who was soaring for God and caused such injury? How many of us have stood by and watched as a wounded brother or sister has tried to find refuge, and we have turned them away without compassion? The church is God's sanctuary—a shelter for those who need to recover and heal from their wounds. The enemy is merciless—a rabid hunter who does not care what carnage he leaves behind. We are to be caretakers of the injured. Some may never fly as they once did, but they will be safe, and their life stories will show others the dangers of the enemy. Others will recover and they will fly again, and it is the church family who will shelter them, help them and cheer them on as they return to flight.

Thought provoker: In our churches, are we the shelter and sanctuary wounded saints need? Let's be the place they can come to heal and recover.

Lord, there are many, many wounded saints in our world today. The enemy is hard at work trying to destroy lives and hurt testimonies. Help us be the shelter and sanctuary they need, not the judges and hunters who continue to hurt them. Let us be agents of Your healing power today. Thank you that You are the Redeemer, the Restorer and the Healer we need. Amen.

Notes/Insights:

More Devotions from Everyday Things

The Dress

Strength and dignity are her clothing, And she smiles at the future.
Proverbs 31:25, NAS

I have come to a decision: shopping is a very difficult task, especially when it comes to ladies' clothes. I "needed" to get a new dress for a special occasion, so my daughter and I made an afternoon "girl-time," and went searching for a new addition to my wardrobe.

We stopped in a couple of department stores, and after three stops, I was getting discouraged. Most of the cute, stylish pieces were either too short in the skirt, or too deep in the neckline. Things were too clingy, too revealing, or just too tacky. We took a break, and stopped for something to eat. As we waited for our food, I began to get a heart-burden—I wanted to stand up and holler, "Ladies, we do not have to settle for this." Of course, I did not, but I did start a conversation with my daughter about self-respect, Godliness and decency. She grinned, and said, "I get it Mom. I don't need to wear something that draws attention in the wrong way. I'm a God's girl, and I want to dress in ways that make Him happy."

I am glad our tween daughter has a good grasp on modesty, and I hope and pray she "gets it" throughout her life. It is not a legalistic or superior attitude with her—it is just a confidence in Whose she is that she does not need to dress skimpy, attract the wrong kind of attention, or define herself by what she wears. Oh, that her confidence would spread throughout the Kingdom. I would love to see girls shed the world's delusion about attraction; that they would, instead, dress with confidence. I would love to see teenage young men and women, married men and women, single guys and girls alike show the world that God's love is the great identity that matters in this life; clothes are just the covering for the shell of the soul. We can dress with the confidence that the people we see in the mirror each morning are God's guys and girls, that His love overflows from us, and that our style reflects His glory. A Godly confidence and integrity that shows strength and enables us to dress as soldiers of the light, these should define our style and fashion, as we decide what covers our skin.

I did finally find the "perfect" dress. The last store we stopped in, my daughter found a cute tunic-style top with a knee length skirt. Not only was it a good fit, it was on sale. Just an added blessing to make sure I would dress with His confidence for that special occasion.

Thought-provoker: Are you dressing in Godly confidence? Make a choice today to dress for the Kingdom.

Lord, help us dress with the confidence that we belong to You, that You are the Author of beauty, and that we can give you glory, and still look fabulous. Amen.

Notes/Insights:

More Devotions from Everyday Things

The Personal Trainer

Likewise the Spirit also helps in our weaknesses. For we do not know what we should pray for as we ought, but the Spirit Himself makes intercession for us with groanings which cannot be uttered. Now He who searches the hearts knows what the mind of the Spirit is, because He makes intercession for the saints according to the will of God.

Romans 8:26-27, NKJV

I have a friend who is a great personal trainer. She is very knowledgeable of the body, how it works, and how to make it burn calories. She is creative in her workout approach and she is very encouraging. The one thing she does not tolerate is groaning. You know, the grunt-like noises that come from your soul as your mind attempts to convince your body you *can* run that extra quarter or you *can* stretch a little farther or you *can* lose two inches around the middle this month. No excuses, grunts or groans; just keep at it. I love her outlook—keep trying and the fitness will come.

In the spiritual realm, we have a Personal Trainer as well. The Scriptures tell us that the Holy Spirit "...helps us with our weaknesses." I think that should translate something like: "He knows how to work out our spiritually weak muscles and bring about spiritual fitness." It also says we don't know how to pray as we should. So many times our hearts and spirits are grieved, or deceived, or just plain selfish and we do not know how to pray correctly. I am so glad our spiritual Personal Trainer knows what to do. It says, "...He makes intercession for us with groanings that cannot be uttered." When I am not able to groan—He can. He searches our hearts, He knows the mind of the Father and He makes intercessions for us—according to the will of God. He knows exactly what it will take for us to grow and become spiritually fit, and He is willing to ask the Father to give it to us. He is willing to take the petitions to the Throne of Mercy for us and He asks God for exactly what we need. A Personal Trainer, on a personal mission, for a person—you. Thank God that He is so willing to make sure we become spiritually fit; let's make sure we get in our spiritual workout with Him today.

Thought provoker: Knowing you have a fantastic Spiritual Personal Trainer, what are you going to do to apply yourself to grow spiritually today? Ask Him for wisdom, guidance, and the determination to get spiritually fit today, and in the days to come.

Lord, thank You for the awesome Personal Trainer You are in my spiritual walk. Strengthen my areas of weakness, and when I do not know how to pray, thank You that I can depend on the Holy Spirit to know exactly what to ask for me. I love You and I worship You today as my Savior, my King and my Trainer. Amen.

Notes/Insights:

Feathers

> He will cover you with His feathers; you will take refuge under His wings. His faithfulness will be a protective shield.
>
> Psalm 91:4, HCSB

It hangs on the wall of the tack room at the barn—a long, turkey tail feather. It is a reminder to the hunters of the grand turkey who wintered on the farm last year, and whom they failed to catch. The feather has the iridescent colors interspersed among the browns and tans. It catches the light when you glance at it from different directions, and it looks impressive on the wall. But, the feather hangs on the wall so it will not be broken, snagged, or pulled apart by wear and tear. After all, it is just a feather, a fragile feather. Feathers are used to make pillows; they are easily broken by small predators, and they are not prized possessions. They are small, insignificant aspects of nature, only noticed because they give birds the ability to fly. Feathers are not weapons, and they are definitely not the foundations for buildings.

But God, in His infinite ability to illustrate His principles, refers to His feathers as our protection—His wings as our refuge. At first glance, that seems to be a very poor illustration; feathers are not enough to protect us and wings are easily broken and destroyed, meaning our refuge from an earthly standpoint is, at the very least, perilous. But not so with God. God, the Creator of the universe, the planner of all our paths, the hope of all our eternities, the Savior of our souls says His feathers are our protection and His wings are our refuge. God's power is so intense, His character so deep, His love so vast for us that it *only takes His feathers* to protect us. Think about it and let that sink in.

God is so strong—His feathers can protect us from the worst of all disasters. His wings are so powerful; He can shield us from the greatest distresses. His love for us is so complete; He does not need to call all the armies of Heaven to defend us—even though they are at His disposal. No, all He needs to be able to care for us are His wings. All He needs to call upon to protect us are His feathers. What seemed at first to be a poor illustration becomes a wonderful picture of hope and peace. What seemed to be perilous at first glance becomes the peaceful truth that gives us balance and refuge in times of trial. With the gentleness of a mother bird, God covers us with His feathers—spreads His wings to shield us, and it is enough. It is enough because He is so powerful that His feathers are enough to protect us from anything. It is enough because He is enough, and nothing—on this earth, in Heaven or anywhere else, will ever be able to get past His wings. Aren't you glad you are covered by the feathers of God?

Thought-provoker: Are you living under the protection of God's wings? If you are, take time to praise Him for His great power and protection over your life. If you are not, why not ask God today to be your refuge from the trials of this life, to be the Savior of your soul and the Hope for your eternity.

Lord, thank You that Your feathers are enough—I need nothing more to protect me from the trials of this life because You are so awesome and powerful. I praise You for Your great care of me. Amen.

Notes/Insights:

More Devotions from Everyday Things

The Red Card

~~~

"Not everyone who says to Me, 'Lord, Lord.' will enter the kingdom of heaven, but only the one who does the will of My Father in heaven. On that day many will say to Me, 'Lord, Lord, didn't we prophesy in Your name, drive out demons in Your name, and do many miracles in Your name?' Then I will announce to them, 'I never knew you. Depart from Me, you lawbreakers.'"

Matthew 7:21-23, HCSB

Both of our sons work as referees at the local soccer fields. They both attended classes to learn all the rules for the league, they passed their certification tests, and then they were issued their uniforms and equipment. In the pocket of each of their shirts, they carry a yellow and a red card. In soccer, these cards are used to alert the players, coaches and spectators that a violation of the rules has occurred and the player being carded is first warned, and then penalized for his/her continued rule-breaking. The yellow card is a warning, but the red card carries the consequences of being removed from the game and not being able to play the next one. It is an interesting process: the referee stands in front of the player, pulls the card out of his pocket, and holds it up for everyone to see. Then, the player's number and infraction is written down and play resumes. Those who were following the rules have nothing to fear from the referee—they play on as if nothing has happened once the referee restarts the game.

There are those in life who think they can play God's game anyway they want. They do not heed the warnings of Scripture, and they break His rules without any sorrow or regret. But God takes notice when we do not follow His Word, and He sends us warnings—through the Spirit's conviction, sound preaching, exhortation from others, or through His Word. If we do not heed those warnings, He may have to "red card" us from the field for awhile to get our attention and to bring us back into full fellowship with Him. When He does sideline us, it is because He wants to restore us, but our stubbornness in refusing to follow His rules makes it necessary to pull us out of the game and set us down until we see our need to repent. Better that He do this now in our lives than for us to get to eternity only to hear Him say, "I never knew you."

We have to play by God's rules. Not because He is a mean-spirited, legalistic, out-to-get-us God—no, He has given us the rules in His Word so we can navigate the field of opponents and be victorious for His glory.

Thought-provoker: Do you need a red card spiritually, or are you following God's rules to play your best game for His glory?

Lord, thank You for Your Word, Your rules, Your guidelines, so we can be the best players we can for Your glory. Thank You for the warnings—help us to heed them. Amen.

Notes/Insights:

More Devotions from Everyday Things

The Helmet

☙❧

Take the helmet of salvation, and the sword of the Spirit, which is God's word.

Ephesians 6:17, HCSB

I know a little bit about helmets. Through a series of unfortunate events in the late spring, my horse and I slid into a metal rail fence. I hit the fence panel head-on as we hit one panel and then slid into the one in front of us. My helmet did its job—it absorbed the blow and protected me from life-threatening injuries. I walked away with some scratches and bruises on my body and I did have a concussion, but I was able to walk out of the hospital, go home and rest, and still "be here" today. My helmet saved my life. Since then, I have noticed some things about helmets. First of all, helmets are not pretty. When I put my riding helmet on, I do not look like a fashion statement for the NY runways, but that helmet also serves a very specific purpose—protection. They are built as a rock with a cushion on the inside to protect the brain and skull. Helmets can also withstand a lot of pressure. New equine regulations have made sure helmets can dissipate pressure across the surface of the helmet and the material it is made of can absorb the shock of a sudden impact.

So, what does this have to do with being God-followers? Ephesians 6 tells us to put on the helmet of salvation. The world does not understand why we need a helmet; they think our helmets are unattractive, ugly, or even ridiculous. But, they are not in the race. They don't understand the fiery darts that are being thrown at us at neck-break speed. They don't understand the sudden impact of a faith crisis when life hits you head-on.

Our helmet serves a very specific purpose. It protects our minds from the massive impacts of grief, loss, death, sickness, spiritual attacks and family problems. Wearing the helmet of salvation doesn't mean we won't feel pain—I still had a physical concussion, but the helmet keeps us from being in a spiritual coma or becoming brain-dead in our faith (2 Timothy 1:7). It protects us and keeps us functioning as believers as we get back up, rest awhile, and then climb back in the saddle for another race.

The security of our salvation can withstand a lot of pressure, just as the helmet absorbs the pressure from impact. In fact, our heavenly helmet will not crack or "blow-out" when we have head-on impacts in life. The safety standards for our spiritual helmet are out-of-this-world specs that will withstand anything, anytime, anywhere in this world.

Just as I need a helmet when I am working with horses, we need our spiritual helmet to give us the protection we need each step of the way.

Thought-provoker: Are you wearing the helmet of salvation and allowing it to absorb the impacts of life?

Lord, thank You that our helmet is strong enough and specifically designed to sustain the pressures of this life and protect us for the life to come. Amen.

Notes/Insights:

More Devotions from Everyday Things

The Veteran

~~~

For I am already being poured out like a drink offering, and the time for my departure is near. I have fought the good fight, I have finished the race, I have kept the faith. Now there is in store for me the crown of righteousness, which the Lord, the righteous Judge, will award to me on that day—and not only to me, but also to all who have longed for his appearing.

2 Timothy 4:6-8, NIV

He was sitting on the side of the road as the parade passed by. This elderly gentleman sat in a lawn chair, dressed in a plain flannel shirt and pants, with glasses and a Veterans' baseball cap. He was quiet, looking somewhat fragile, but he seemed to be enjoying the antics of the clowns and the music of the marching band as it passed.

But, when the military unit marched in procession—he stood up. It was an ordeal for him to get to his feet, but he rocked in his chair until his momentum got him to his feet, and then he stood there, at attention with a proper salute for those young men and women in uniform as they marched by. He did not move—standing firm and strong in his stance. His fragileness was overtaken by a determination to honor those who were serving. The leader of the unit walked over, said something to the elderly man, who quickly dropped his salute to shake the man's hand. The elderly man seemed moved by the words of the unit leader. As he sat down, his family moved in closer to ask what had transpired. "He said thank you for your service," was all the elderly man said and then he sat with emotion-filled eyes and watched the rest of the parade.

Oh, what a moment for my family to experience. The honor bestowed by a veteran, and the gratefulness of a current member of the military. The veteran—the one who had fought the fight and the unit leader who was leading the charge—were together for a moment and a handshake. This is what I picture when I read Paul's words in the passage today. Here, Paul, the veteran, is honoring Timothy with a testimonial and a charge. Timothy was in the midst of the battle; Paul was getting ready to retire to Glory. If the two had been together, I think they would have had a moment's conversation and a handshake.

In today's rush and hustle of life, we need to take time to thank the veterans of the faith that have gone before us and to let them know how much we appreciate their sacrifices and examples for us to follow, and we need to honor those who are in the battle right now.

Thought-provoker: Are you grateful for those who are veterans of the faith? Are you encouraging the soldiers of faith today?

Lord, thank You for the veterans and the soldiers who are fighting the good fight of faith. Please help us to support and encourage those who are before us and behind us on this journey called life. Amen.

Notes/Insights:

More Devotions from Everyday Things

The Roadblock

Make me to know your ways, O Lord; teach me your paths. Lead me in your truth and teach me, for you are the God of my salvation; for you I wait all the day long.

Psalm 25:4-5, ESV

Teenage drivers have a tough job. Not only are they learning to control a ton of heavy metal and motor, but they also have to navigate where they are going. Our oldest son was doing a good job of doing both the Wednesday afternoon we were heading to church. We came to the last light before the intersection for our church, and there was a police vehicle, lights on, and an officer standing outside the car flagging people to take a detour. We pulled up to take our turn, and asked if it were possible to get to the church. "No, the accident is right before you get there," was her reply. We thanked her, and took the detour.

The problem with the detour was we were not sure where to go. It was a distraction from the route we had planned to take. We followed the cars in front of us, until I saw the name of a road that was familiar. We took it. It took us a little out-of-the-way, but at least it was familiar and we knew it would get us back to where we wanted to be. As we drove, we noticed the farmland, the openness, and the beauty that was afforded to those natural back roads. The traffic wasn't as bad as the main drive either. We found a moment of beauty because we had to navigate to go another way.

In our spiritual journeys, sometimes there are roadblocks. We have a designated route—a routine that helps us stay on track and keeps us focused. When circumstances upset our routine, we have to navigate around them. We need to go to God's Word and find something familiar—something that helps us to get back where we want to be. Those detours help us to find openness, beauty—a breath of fresh air from the main drives of life. The detours remind us that God is still in control, and He knows we need a break from the heavy traffic of the mundane, so He detours us to a place of peace and quiet, and there we find a renewed vision of Who He is.

We did eventually get to the church; a power pole had landed across the road and needed to be replaced. It was a good reminder that every now and then, it is good to take a different route to enjoy the change of scenery and slow down so we can be reminded of God's faithfulness—even in the navigation.

Thought-provoker: How do you handle roadblocks? Ask God to reveal the beauty you may be missing on your regular route of the routine.

Lord, thank You for roadblocks that require us to go a different way and discover the adventure, beauty and peace You have for us. Help us to see the opportunities, instead of the inconveniences. Amen.

Notes/Insights:

Laser Tag

Be serious. Be alert. Your adversary the Devil is prowling around like a roaring lion, looking for anyone he can devour. Resist him and be firm in the faith, knowing that the same sufferings are being experienced by your fellow believers throughout the world.

I Peter 5:8-9, HCSB

We love to play laser tag. For birthdays, or other special occasions, we enjoy getting a group of family and friends together and heading out to the local Laser Tag warehouse. Once there, we split into teams, we "gear up," grab our weapons and head into the mazes of darkness, dry ice and mirrors to fend off the other team and enjoy bragging rights until our next meeting.

When we first get into the maze, though, we have to adjust. After a few moments, we begin to see shadows moving across the room, and small red lights that are targets on the other team's gear begin to become more visible. We can hear footsteps above and below us in the maze, and detecting the trigger sound from a laser gun becomes necessary as we dodge others' attempts to hit our vest targets or deactivate our guns for a few seconds with a direct hit.

What isn't so obvious is who the enemy is. We are all dressed in dark clothing. We are trying to avoid direct lines of fire, and sneaking through mazes of obstacles and mirrors makes it tough to determine who we should be firing at. It takes time to figure out who is on each team and which guns we should be aiming to take out and which ones are our allies.

Our spiritual walk is a lot like that laser tag game. There are teams—God's and Satan's. There are opponents, and we have to figure out who is the enemy, and who are our allies. Satan is looking to devour us, and our focus should be on defeating him through the name, power and blood of Jesus Christ. But, we have to be sure we are not aiming to take someone else out in our line-of-fire. We need to see our enemy clearly and we need to aim our weapons at him, and leave our allies alone.

How do we do this? We use our spiritual weapons of the Word, faith and prayer to attack the enemy by going to God and asking Him to fight for us. We do not tear down others who are in the fight with us, but we encourage them and keep our aim off of their lives. We work together to advance the Kingdom of Light, and we make sure our aim is against the kingdom of darkness and not another poor soul fighting his way through the maze of life and trying to come out victorious as well.

Thought-provoker: Who are you aiming your spiritual weapons at today? Are you sure you have the right enemy in your sights?

Lord, thank You for the victory we have in You. Please help us to keep our spiritual weapons aimed at the enemy and not at each other. Amen.

Notes/Insights:

The Bee Sting

But you have not so learned Christ, if indeed you have heard Him and have been taught by Him, as the truth is in Jesus: that you put off, concerning your former conduct, the old man which grows corrupt according to the deceitful lusts, and be renewed in the spirit of your mind, and that you put on the new man which was created according to God, in true righteousness and holiness.

Ephesians 4:20-24 NKJV

I am allergic to bee stings. I found this out when I was a young girl playing in the backyard. A bee landed on my foot and stung me, and in just a few minutes, my foot and ankle were swollen. As a college student, it happened again, only this time I swelled and broke out in hives. One more time as an adult, and I felt my throat get tight. That was enough of a warning for me; I now carry an emergency pack to interrupt the allergic reaction.

My carelessness came about because I did not keep up my vigil against bee stings. I let things slide—I didn't always carry the antidote with me because it had been so long since I had been stung. But, sitting there in my friend's car as she drove me to the pharmacy, I wish I had it. We had been boating and picnicking on the lakeside, and a bee decided he liked the same spot where I sat to eat my lunch. When I interrupted his lunch, he interrupted mine. I realized quickly that the burning sensation on my leg was from a bee sting, and I reached in my purse to find the emergency pack. It wasn't there. I had gone for so long without a sting that I had left it at home in the cabinet. Thankfully, my friend has a nursing degree and she understood the urgency of getting something in my system, so off we went to the pharmacy. If only I had put the emergency pack in the right place, I would have had it when I needed it.

Spiritually, we can get careless. We can let things slide, not keeping the essentials where they need to be. We can be lulled into laziness by the seemingly long times between trials. We think we are doing ok, we have risen above our need to be diligent; life will be ok without all that preparedness. Then, when we least expect it, our "old man" stings us. We reach for the emergency pack—the essentials of our Christian walk that kept us diligent, consistent and strong, only we have left them at home. Our Bible is on the shelf, our prayer life is inconsistent, and our old man has grown corrupt and deceitful. Fortunately, God steps in—much like my dear friend did—and takes us to a place to get what we need. It may be an altar after a powerful message on repentance, or a time of trial that leads us back to the consistency and diligence to rid ourselves of the old man and put on the new one--the spiritual one who depends on God and stays diligent in His Word to be ready and live righteously.

Thought-provoker: Have you been careless in your spiritual walk? Take time to put the essentials back in place and spend time with God to be sure you are being diligent in your relationship with Him.

Lord, help me not to be careless in my walk with You. Please keep me diligent, consistent and faithful through Your power and for Your glory. Amen.

Notes/Insights:

More Devotions from Everyday Things

The Huddle

Therefore, I remind you to keep ablaze the gift of God that is in you through the laying on of my hands. For God has not given us a spirit of fearfulness, but one of power, love, and sound judgment.

1 Timothy 1:6-7, ESV

For this gospel I was appointed a herald, apostle, and teacher, and that is why I suffer these things. But I am not ashamed, because I know the One I have believed in and am persuaded that He is able to guard what has been entrusted to me until that day.

2 Timothy 1:11-12, ESV

With four high school rivalries in our area, football is a big deal. We can see the lights of one of the fields from our house, and boys in our neighborhood are on the team. I like to watch football—a game that combines strength and strategy; the pushing and the passing, all make for a great time of cheering and entertainment.

But, what if the teams never left the huddle? What if the teams stayed circled up, facing each other? They could keep encouraging each other, calling plays and making plans, but they must break the huddle at some point and square up against the opposing team on the line of scrimmage. They have to leave the comfort of the huddle in order to play the game.

Now, I bet some of the players—especially the linesmen whose job is to push back the opposing team so their team goes forward to score—would love to stay in that comfortable huddle. They enjoy the encouragement and face-to-face contact with their own players. But, they know the huddle is not where the game is won—it's not where the opponent is pushed back and it is not where victory is attained.

We like our huddles, spiritually speaking. We enjoy being with others who believe as we do. We can encourage each other for days on end at conferences, meetings, and worship services. We have been called, however, to the front lines of the battle for men's souls. We are to be pushing back the forces of darkness with our testimonies, prayers, courage and witnessing to win the lost for Christ and gain victories for the Kingdom of God.

Don't misunderstand; there is a time and a place for huddles in the football game. The team needs those moments to encourage one another and to know what the call is so the play is successful. We need those times too, but if we only ever stay in the huddle and never experience the battle—we are not winning. God calls us over comers—let's get to the front line.

Thought-provoker: Have you stayed in the huddle too long, or are you battling for the kingdom?

Lord, thank You for the times when I need the huddle to encourage me and keep me strong in the faith. But, thank You that You have chosen me as a part of Your team, and You trust me to help forward Your kingdom. Help me to do my part on the frontlines today. Amen.

Notes/Insights:

More Devotions from Everyday Things

The Tight-Rope Walker

My help comes from the LORD, who made heaven and earth. He will not let your foot be moved; he who keeps you will not slumber.
Psalm 121:2, ESV

I had the privilege of briefly rubbing shoulders, literally, with a tight-rope walker on vacation last summer. We bumped into each other in a crowd as we were exiting the theater where he and his family had just done a show. He smiled and thanked us for coming, and then moved to the autograph table.

The show had been great—spotlights on poles, bicycles, and chairs all being stacked on tight wires as people climbed on each others' shoulders and balanced high in the air. There was a moment during the show, though, when they showed a video of the lead walker going across Niagara Falls. The wind, the spray, the intense focus on his face, and then the moment when he reached the other side and everyone cheered. He had done what many considered to be the impossible.

I was intrigued enough that I went home and did some research about Niagara Falls tightrope walkers. Everyone who watched the tightrope walkers was thrilled by their feats, but there was one legend that caught my attention. A tightrope walker walked across the rope, first by himself, then with a wheelbarrow. Everyone was impressed. Then, he asked the crowd if he was a good tightrope walker. "Yes, yes, of course you are." came the response. Then, he challenged one, anyone, to get in the wheelbarrow and go across with him. No one responded. It was stunningly quiet. Then, one young boy stepped forward and said, "I will do it." He got in the wheelbarrow and everyone watched in amazement as the tightrope walker safely transported the young fellow across and back the rope again. The crowd erupted into applause and the boy was hailed a hero. When asked why he did it, the boy simply replied, "I knew he could do it—he's my dad."

Now, whether that legend is true or not, the principle goes deep. The boy knew he could trust the man who put out the challenge. He knew his father would be safe and bring him back to land without harm. Others standing there were impressed by the man's feats, but they were not impressed enough to get into the wheelbarrow—to accept the tightrope walker's challenge. Many in life are this way with God, the Creator. He has proven He is worthy of our trust, worthy to be our Savior, but some refuse to accept the challenge to receive Him by faith (John 1:12). The boy did exactly what the tightrope walker challenged, and the boy received the thrill of a lifetime. When we accept Jesus as Savior by faith and place our lives in His hands, we receive the promise of His presence in this life and the joy of an eternity with Him in glory—and it doesn't get any better than that.

Thought-provoker: Have you accepted Christ's offer of salvation by faith?

Lord, thank You for being my Savior, and that it doesn't depend on me, it is all about faith in You. Amen.

Notes/Insights:

More Devotions from Everyday Things

The Faucet

I give thanks to my God for every remembrance of you, always praying with joy for all of you in my every prayer, because of your partnership in the gospel from the first day until now. I am sure of this, that He who started a good work in you will carry it on to completion until the day of Christ Jesus.

Philippians 1:4-6, HCSB

Knowing that I am not mechanically-inclined, I should have just left it well enough alone, but the shower kept dripping. The dripping went on for awhile, was getting progressively worse and I grew impatient. I took a pair of pliers to the handle—and wound up creating a bigger leak inside the wall. The plumber had to come; and when he was finished there was a two foot square hole in the wall in the living room. That led to having to paint a wall—then an entire room because we could not find the matching paint. One thing led to another. One problem led to more work. One issue created several—all because I tried to help the process along.

Don't we do the same thing to God? He is at work in our lives, but the process is taking too long, so we try to help, and before we know it—we've created a bigger mess. We want Him to fix the things in our lives that drip—those little frustrations that drive us crazy, and we wind up with a heart full of broken pieces that need to be put back together.

Wouldn't it be so much better just to let the Master do his work? The plumber fixed the leak in no time—less than a few hours, and the shower would have been as good as new without the extra work of patching the wall and painting the living room. What if we allowed God to do His work in His time and agreed to His timetable instead of rushing ahead of His ideas? What if we were willing to sit quietly as He worked a miracle of peace and renewal in our hearts? We need to understand that He has the blueprint and He knows exactly what needs to be improved upon in our lives. He also knows how much time it will take, and He knows we need to develop the endurance and perseverance, and yes, the patience, that come from gradual progress. He knows instant gratification does not foster gratefulness—our memories are too easily distracted. But something that takes time becomes a beautiful reminder of His work in our lives that won't be easily forgotten.

Thought-provoker: What improvement is God working in your life that is taking time? Are you working with the Lord, allowing Him to do the work in His time or are you prying into the process and creating more of a mess?

Lord, I am sorry that I get impatient with Your perfect work. Please help me to agree to Your timing and submit to Your process, for this is the best way. Amen.

Notes/Insights:

More Devotions from Everyday Things

The Scar

༄༅

"Therefore strengthen your tired hands and weakened knees, and make straight paths for your feet, so that what is lame may not be dislocated, but healed instead. Pursue peace with everyone, and holiness—without it no one will see the Lord. Make sure that no one falls short of the grace of God and that no root of bitterness springs up, causing trouble and by it, defiling many."

Hebrews 12:12-15, HCSB

It was one of those crazy moments. I was cleaning and organizing the storage area, and a bungee cord that was holding equipment on a shelf, let loose. I saw it coming and I ducked, but it grazed my eyebrow and left its mark. Blood gushed and I grabbed a towel to stop it. Once I got the bleeding stopped, I put a butterfly bandage on it. Of course, it left a scar, so a few days after the scab fell off; I started putting scar reducer on it. I wanted that scar to be as minimal as possible, and I was willing to work at making it go away. After all, the scar was on my face, and I did not want it to be more noticeable than my eyes or my smile.

That scar was stubborn, though. It took work, and diligence, to get it to heal. But, one day when I looked in the mirror, it wasn't the first thing that I saw. The scar had diminished, and it was not the prominent feature I noticed.

Bitterness is a lot like that scar. Crazy moments in life—a word said in anger or a relationship broken by hurtful words or actions—cut at our hearts and leave wounds. Sometimes, we gush, emotionally, and it takes grace to stop the emotional bleeding. The bitterness becomes obvious, it's noticeable, and it takes work to get rid of it. We have to pursue peace with everyone, and holiness. It is not enough to just admit the bitterness is there, or to close our eyes and pretend it is not there. It will take work to change our thinking, to change our attitudes and to go away from the hurt and bitterness. We have to forgive the ones who have hurt us, and we have to lean in hard to feel the grace of God at work in our lives to help us heal. But, as we apply those attributes of peace and holiness to our lives, we minimize the scarring that is caused by sin, hurts, and consequences. We apply forgiveness as the salve to heal those hurts, and the bitterness cannot take root and become the prominent feature of our lives. And, one day, we look at ourselves in the mirror and realize that the hurt and the bitterness are no longer prominent in our lives, because God—the Great Physician—is so good.

Thought-provoker: Is there a scar in your heart that needs more healing? Ask God to heal it, and be willing to do what it takes to cooperate with Him.

Lord, thank You for healing our scars with Your grace, peace, and holiness. Amen.

Notes/Insights:

Noisy Dogs

"Do all things without complaining and disputing, that you may become blameless and harmless, children of God without fault in the midst of a crooked and perverse generation, among whom you shine as lights in the world, holding fast the word of life, so that I may rejoice in the day of Christ that I have not run in vain or labored in vain."

Philippians 2:14-16, NKJV

Ava has celebrated another birthday with us. She is officially out of the puppy stage and has begun to show her maturity. Most of the time now, she accepts her role as companion, lays by our feet when we are sitting in the living room, or on a pillow in the corner when I am busy in the office. She is also a good guardian. She alerts us to noises outside, and she barks at the door when someone pulls in the driveway. She's still a little quirky, but we love her and accept her uniqueness as a member of our family.

One thing, however, that drives me absolutely bonkers is her reaction to our neighbor's dogs. The neighbor's dogs live behind a privacy fence, a fence on which a cat loves to cross. The two dogs fly into a frenzy when the cat arrives, and they continue to carry on long after the cat makes his leap of exit to another yard. The two dogs barking and yelping is enough to contend with, but Ava adds to the annoyance by sitting at the back window—and whining. Her pitiful, persistent whine. She stares out the window and watches what the other dogs are doing, and whines. It is so annoying that more than once I have firmly called her from the window with an emphatic, "No. Come here, now."

The passage today tells us, "no whining." Even when others are all worked up about something—a cat on the fence—we are to remain calm, blameless and pure children of God. We are not to sit and stare at the situation and complain. Why not? Because complaining mars us—it stains our character and goes against God's good pleasure. God doesn't tell us it is ok to complain a little; He tells us not to do it at all. It's an emphatic, "No," just like my command to Ava to come away from the window.

So, what should we do when others get in a tizzy about a cat on a fence, and we cannot do anything about it? Go sit by our heavenly Father's feet and, just like Ava, enjoy the blessings of being a part of His wonderful family. Listen to His voice as He tells you to come away from the window of the world and sit in His presence. You will be at peace in obedience.

Thought-provoker: Will you commit to obeying God and not whine or complain? Count your blessings instead.

Lord, help us to follow Your command to not complain at all. As hard as it is, You have the power for us to obey. Thank You. Amen.

Notes/Insights:

More Devotions from Everyday Things

The Filling

"I am the true vine, and my Father is the gardener. He cuts off every branch in me that bears no fruit, while every branch that does bear fruit he prunes so that it will be even more fruitful. You are already clean because of the word I have spoken to you. Remain in me, as I also remain in you. No branch can bear fruit by itself; it must remain in the vine. Neither can you bear fruit unless you remain in me."

John 15:1-4, HCSB

Our dentist is a great guy, but that did not make it any easier. After a perfect track record for over thirty years—I got my first cavity. And not just one—an undiagnosed physical condition had caused deterioration in my teeth, and now it needed to be fixed. I was not looking forward to the appointment, but I knew I had to go. A trip to my primary care physician had revealed the problem, medication was prescribed and monitored, and now it was time to correct the cavities and restore my smile.

The dentist worked carefully. He numbed my mouth, and then he removed the decay with a drill. He cleaned the tooth, dried it, applied epoxy and the filling material. He set it, heated it, smoothed the rough edges and *voila*. My teeth were clean, filled and ready for use again. No pain; no more decay. The dentist had cut away the decay and put a filling in its place.

God the Father works like the dentist in our spiritual lives. He prunes away the decay of old habits and traditions to allow us to grow in a different direction. He fills those gaps in our spiritual walk with new things that will make us effective and useful in new ministries. He works carefully, removing only what is necessary, and making sure the decay in our spiritual life is completely cut away. He replaces it with spiritual growth and fruit. He smooths the rough edges in our character, and makes it possible for us to smile again. Going through the process is not enjoyable, but the results of a stronger faith and effective ministry to God's glory make it all worthwhile.

Thought-provoker: Are there areas of decay in your life that need pruning? Are you allowing God to grow and change you, or are you holding onto spiritual cavities?

Lord, please fill my life with the good things, and allow me to give up the things that are causing gaps in my spiritual life. Please don't allow me to hold onto my spiritual cavities. Amen.

Notes/Insights:

The Hole

"Don't collect for yourselves treasure on earth, where moth and rust destroy and where thieves break in and steal. But collect for yourselves treasures in heaven, where neither moth nor rust destroys, and where thieves don't break in and steal. For where your treasure is, there your heart will be also."

Matthew 6:19-20, HCSB

After the heat of a long summer, the weather finally broke. I woke up to a chill in the air and eager anticipation. The first cold snap deemed it a necessity to wear my favorite sweater. I dug into the back of my closet to get it—a cute pink sweater with a crochet overlay. I am not typically a "girlie-girl," but this sweater was feminine and cute, and it fit right in all the right places.

As I pulled it out, my smile melted away. There in the middle of the front panel—a hole. I took the sweater to my sewing table and tried three different ways to fix the hole. The hole seemed to reappear, no matter how I tried to fix it. Something had frayed the fibers in that one spot, and no amount of sewing would hold them together anymore. My sweater was ruined by some sneaky pest—a moth, time, or perhaps some kind of chemical, and now I could not wear it. I sighed as I put it down and then went digging in my closet for another sweater to wear, because it was still chilly, and I had to find something to help me stay warm.

What if—what if things didn't wear out? What if colors didn't fade, or fabrics didn't dry rot? What if tools lasted, and houses didn't get leaks? What if we were always healthy, happy and got what we wanted in this life? I believe we would think life is more permanent than we should. I think we would become secure in the temporary, and satisfy our souls with the physical. We would neglect eternal values and settle for present pleasures. But, houses do need repairs; things do wear out, and our favorite sweaters do get holes. God changes our circumstances so our hearts do not settle for the here and now; He allows our hearts to yearn for something more. So much more, because we yearn for Him—we yearn for all of His power, presence, and peace and we learn to be secure in His love. His eternal love that never wears out, fades, or gets holes in it. He is the permanent favorite our hearts seek—and He will keep us warm not matter how chilly the day may be.

Thought-provoker: Where is your focus? Is Christ your soul's favorite, or are you settling for something far less? Take time to truly think about where your heart's desire is today.

Lord, please be my soul's favorite and my heart's desire. Consume me with Your permanence, secure my heart's devotion steadfastly in Your eternal love. Only then, will my spirit be truly satisfied and my soul content. Amen.

Notes/Insights:

More Devotions from Everyday Things

The Catcher's Glove

∽◈∾

Where can I go from Your Spirit? Or where can I flee from Your presence? If I ascend into heaven, You are there; If I make my bed in hell, behold, You are there. If I take the wings of the morning, And dwell in the uttermost parts of the sea, Even there Your hand shall lead me, And Your right hand shall hold me."

Psalm 139:7-10, NKJV

I love to watch my son's team play baseball, but there is no way I would play a certain position. Outfield—ok, I may not have the strongest arm, but I could at least get the ball to the cut-off player. Infield—the team would probably not have me play, but I could hold my own with a few good fielding attempts and a few good base throws. But, even with all the protective gear, to be the catcher--to squat behind the plate as a ball is pitched at eighty or ninety miles an hour, and be expected not only to stop it, but also to catch it in a glove—well, let's just say I am not that brave or coordinated.

But, there he was, pitch after pitch. Consistently catching the ball and returning it to the pitcher. Curve ball, he caught it. Outside pitch, he reached out and got it. Fast ball down the middle, he made sure it went straight into the glove. When the ball was hit, he jumped up and prepared himself to defend the plate. He never seemed to get tired. He enjoyed his job as the catcher for my son's ball team and he even joked with the umpire in a respectful way. It never seemed to occur to him that the ball could become an instrument of pain or injury if he missed it; he just kept catching.

In life, I am glad God says He is willing to play the catcher's position. He is never surprised by life's curve balls of circumstances and relationships. He is able to reach the outside pitches of grief and trials. He catches the fast balls that seek to strike us out. He doesn't miss a pitch. In our passage today, He tells us there is nowhere we can go that He is not already there, and He will hold us with His right hand. He will catch whatever life throws at us, and He will consistently be there to defend us. He never gets tired and He enjoys His position as our heavenly Father. He is always prepared, always ready. No matter what may come, He will keep catching.

Thought-provoker: Are you trusting God to catch for you, or are you trying to do life on your own?

Lord, thank You that You are able to catch anything that comes in this life, and You do not miss. Thank You for handling the difficulties of life and consistently defending me. Thank You for allowing me the privilege to be on Your team. Amen.

Notes/Insights:

The Pop-up Camper

"Let not your heart be troubled; you believe in God, believe also in Me. In My Father's house are many mansions; if it were not so, I would have told you. I go to prepare a place for you. And if I go and prepare a place for you, I will come again and receive you to Myself; that where I am, there you may be also. And where I go you know, and the way you know."

John 14:1-4, NKJV

We like to travel. We enjoy going to new places, seeing the sights, doing things together as a family, and making great memories. It is fun to go to a new city and try new things, see new sights and meet new people. In order to take trips affordably, we bought a pop-up camper. When we arrive at our temporary new home, we set the camper on blocks, pop it open, unroll the canopy, set up the chairs, connect the hoses and plug in the electricity. We then have a place where all of us can sleep, eat, laugh, play games and have fun. We can go sight-seeing during the day, and come back to our camper for peace and quiet at night. We meet new people, make friends, help each other when we can, and live in a community for a time. But, it's temporary. After the week is over, we have to take it all back down, roll up the canopy, disconnect the hoses, unplug wires, and wind the camper back down to travel home. The camper is great for a week or two of vacation, but I wouldn't want to live in it year-round. Even after a great vacation, home is where we look forward to going. It's where we belong.

Our lives here on earth are like that pop-up camper. We set up "camp," enjoy being together, and make memories, but it's only temporary. We can learn new things and take in new sights. We do our best to make this life memorable—to enjoy the moments together, meet new people, make new friends, help where we can, and be a part of a community where we can make a difference and have fun. We take time to tell people about our permanent home—Heaven—and our glorious Savior, Jesus Christ, who has purchased us with His blood, and how He is building our new home with His own hands. We know there is a better, permanent home to get to, and when the hour is right, God will tell us to break down the campsite, because it's time to go home. It's time to pack up the temporary and travel to forever with Him. Because that is where we belong—and what we are looking forward to.

Thought-provoker: Are you looking forward to your forever home in Heaven, or are you putting too much emphasis on the campsite here?

Lord, thank You that You are building us a forever home in Heaven that is more than we can imagine. Please help us to enjoy the temporary campsite here, but not get too attached. Amen.

Notes/Insights:

More Devotions from Everyday Things

The Island

For as the body is one and has many parts, and all the parts of that body, though many, are one body—so also is Christ. For we were all baptized by one Spirit into one body—whether Jews or Greeks, whether slaves or free—and we were all made to drink of one Spirit. So the body is not one part but many.

I Corinthians 12:12-14, HCSB

I love reruns. The old television shows with clean comedy and good language give me a reprieve and laughter from a busy schedule. I don't get to watch very often, so I tend to choose carefully, based on the "laugh factor." Gilligan's Island is a sure-fire hit for a good laugh. The antics of Gilligan, the goofiness of Skipper, the wacky inventions of the professor, and the situation comedy of the others bring a smile, and my kids' eye-rolls at some of the jokes make me laugh out loud.

Seven people on an island. They went out for a pleasure cruise, but they wound up stuck on an island for several seasons—alone and isolated. They thought they were going to enjoy a day, and it turned out that they were caught in the storm of their lives. How many times does that happen to us spiritually? We let our guard down—after all, things are going well—the sun is shining, and there is no indication of a battle or a storm on the horizon. We go out for a "pleasure cruise," and put the boat on autopilot. All of a sudden, we find ourselves in the fight of our lives. And, if we're not careful, we will wind up on a spiritual island. We feel shipwrecked, and we think there is no way to get back home. We cut ourselves off from people who can help us, choosing instead to commiserate with others who are also stuck on that island.

When we find ourselves there on that spiritual island—isolated, alone and miserable because a storm capsized our walk, or a battle wounded us—we need to send up the rescue flare, ask God to forgive us, and get back with the family who will love us and accept us again. We need to go home. The island was a great backdrop for Gilligan, but it is a miserable place for the children of God. Get rescued, and go back to the family where you belong—and do it now.

Thought-provoker: Are you on a spiritual island, isolated and alone? What do you need to do to get back with the family of God and make things right with Him?

Lord, thank You that Your family is not an island, but a group of believers who love You and love each other. Thank You that I can always come back home, and I don't have to be isolated and alone, even if it's my fault that I find myself on a spiritual island. Lord, You are so good. Amen.

Notes/Insights:

The Lease

> Then Job arose and tore his robe and shaved his head, and he fell to the ground and worshiped. He said, "Naked I came from my mother's womb, And naked I shall return there. The LORD gave and the LORD has taken away. Blessed be the name of the LORD." Through all this Job did not sin nor did he blame God.
>
> Job 1:20-22, NAS

Leases are agreements between two individuals that one will loan something to the other for a period of time. They can be for houses, equipment, even livestock. The lease allows one person to benefit from loaning, and the other to benefit from borrowing. The tricky part about a lease is the borrower does not own the object being borrowed. The leaser keeps ownership.

God owns everything. He created it all, He keeps it all going (Colossians 1:16-17). As long as we keep the right perspective, we can keep from having a tight grip on the things that have been loaned to us. But, when we start to think we own it; when we start to believe that it is ours, problems come. We tighten our grip; our expectations become too great, and we usually wind up being disappointed. Something happens, the lease is over, and we lose the thing that we thought was making us happy. We become disillusioned, upset, bitter.

How different it would be if we kept the right perspective. "Through all this Job did not sin, nor did he blame God." It's easy to read those words, but it is so hard to picture. Job lost his wealth, his children, his health and his well-being. It didn't take a lifetime of gradually letting go, it happened all at once. And yet, he was able to hold onto the right perspective, not the things. He fell on his face and worshiped—yes, worshiped—God. He didn't beg for different circumstances, he didn't ask for a different outcome. He worshiped God. Worship is the decision to revere, love and be devoted to one of deity. There is only one God, and Job chose to worship Him at the moment of his toughest anguish and greatest heartache. Job did not blame God, and Job was not privy to the conversations in Heaven and knew he had to "hang in there" for the sake of God's character. All he knew was his life—the blessings and all that came with them—were a lease from God and when it was all said and done, Job honored the lease. And God honored him: "The LORD blessed the latter part of Job's life more than the former part" (Job 42:12). He is the same God, yesterday, today and forever.

Thought-provoker: Are you grasping your blessings too tightly and are you too focused on them, or are you thanking the Lord for them and using them as He sees fit?

Lord, You own it all. Thank You for sharing with me. Help me not to hold on too tightly, but be grateful for all the things You have given. Amen.

Notes/Insights:

More Devotions from Everyday Things

The Berry Bush

I shall not die, but I shall live, and recount the deeds of the Lord.

PSALM 118:17, ESV

But the fruit of the Spirit is love, joy, peace, patience, kindness, goodness, faithfulness, gentleness, self-control; against such things there is no law. And those who belong to Christ Jesus have crucified the flesh with its passions and desires.

Galatians 5:22-23, ESV

I sat in the car in tears. The unexpected news that a dear friend was battling a serious illness was sinking in. As I waited to pick up my son, I had cried out to God, earnestly seeking healing and restoration for her. A breeze blew past and I looked up to see a bush—withered and dry from the cold winter, but bearing berries, nonetheless.

As I sat and watched, I noticed the bush was covered with berries. Even though the leaves were gone and the stems were not vibrant with lush green color, the berries were still drooping from the stems and weighing the bush down.

As I thought about my friend, I realized her life was like that bush. Even though a physical illness was withering her vibrancy, her life was still bearing fruit for God's glory. She was walking through the ordeal of treatment, isolation, and a scaled-back life with faith, dignity and grace. She was displaying the gifts of grace God had entrusted to her during this trial, and her life was "weighed down" by the fruit God was producing through her faith. She trusted Him—even when there were a myriad of reasons not to.

That night, the berry bush gave me hope. Just as it stood, bearing fruit in the frigid cold, my friend's illness was not going to stop her from being the woman of faith I had come to know and love. Even in the midst of a cold winter, physically speaking, she would continue to bear fruit for the Lord and for others to see.

Just as she remained fruitful in her circumstances, so should each of us. Our trials, our winters are all different. Some of us have physical trials, others handle tough circumstances; still others deal with grief and loss. But, not matter our winters, we can continue to share God's love, grace and glory through each season, and watch as He blesses us with fruit to bear. We go through seasons when we are not lush and green with lots of activity and productivity, but we can continue to allow the Lord to produce the fruits of the Spirit—love, joy, peace, patience, kindness, gentleness, meekness, faith and self-control—in our lives no matter what the season in which we may find ourselves.

Thought-provoker: Is the season in your life a difficult one? Are you allowing the Lord to produce fruit, no matter what season you may be in?

Lord, thank You for changing seasons of life, and as we journey on, please help us to remember that You can produce fruit in all seasons—even winter—when we allow You to determine what fruit that should be. Amen.

Notes/Insights:

The Hidden Painting

~~~
Therefore, if anyone is in Christ, he is a new creation; old things have passed away, and look, new things have come. Everything is from God, who reconciled us to Himself through Christ and gave us the ministry of reconciliation: That is, in Christ, God was reconciling the world to Himself, not counting their trespasses against them, and He has committed the message of reconciliation to us.
~~~
2 Corinthians 5:17-19, HCSB

I have to confess something—I love to watch restoration television. You know, the shows where they find a painting in an old frame at a yard or rummage sale and the finder's curiosity gets the best of them. They start researching and, eventually, they wind up at an art gallery or museum where the art conservator realizes there may be a far more valuable work of art than the finder first realized. With permission, the conservator starts to meticulously work on a corner of the painting, and—if his/her hunch is correct, they begin to reveal a masterpiece underneath. After hours of carefully precise and painstaking work, the original artwork is revealed and the true worth of the painting is assessed.

Watching the process—from the find to the final reveal—always interests me. The best part of the show, for me, is watching the conservator go to work. Those fine, precise tools, along with the knowledge of how to go about revealing the artwork underneath, are just fascinating. The conservator is patient, diligent and careful as he/she slowly rubs away the top painting, the facade, and washes away the less valuable work with the right mixture of chemicals and elbow grease until a truly magnificent piece is revealed underneath.

Maybe I am so fascinated by the process because I understand it from a personal perspective. God, the loving Master Artist, created each one of us as a masterpiece, but the smudges of the world, and the work of sin in our lives, covers up that masterpiece. Our true worth in Christ is hidden and we do not show the world our true value. When we come to Jesus for redemption, He makes us new. Just like a Master Conservator, He wipes away the façade that covers His artwork underneath and allows us to show forth His glory and be magnificent pieces of beauty for a world that desperately wants to see the hand of God in the world around them. He continues to make things new—He works diligently and carefully until our smudges and pitiful attempts to paint our life-meanings are washed off and the original piece He had planned for us shows through. Our true value can only be assessed when the Master Artist's work can be seen. It is our job, then, to make sure the world sees His work. After all, masterpieces are to be on display so others can see them and become interested in the Artist.

Thought-provoker: Have you allowed God to rub off the façade? Are you living as a masterpiece for Him?

Lord, thank You for making masterpieces—even us. Amen.

Notes/Insights:

More Devotions from Everyday Things

The Leash

"Teacher, which is the great commandment in the Law?" And he said to him, "You shall love the Lord your God with all your heart and with all your soul and with all your mind. This is the great and first commandment. And a second is like it: You shall love your neighbor as yourself."

Matthew 22:36-39, ESV

I am impressed with my neighbor. Actually, we are very blessed to have good neighbors all along the street where we live, but one in particular impressed me with her dog-training abilities. You see, her dog will walk with her without a leash. Ava and I are not even able to attempt that feat yet. Our neighbor has a cute, rambunctious terrier, but the moment they set out the door, her dog walks by her side. If her dog gets distracted, she simply says, "Distraction. No, come here," and her dog trots right back to follow at her heels.

I have tried to do that with Ava, within the boundaries of our own backyard. I let her off the leash to play fetch with a ball one day. She chased every leaf that blew and every bird that fluttered by. My hopeless calls for her to heel and to come were totally unheeded. She was determined to enjoy every distraction possible, and she ran as far from me as our backyard would allow. She ran through the bushes by the house, along the fence line behind the swing set, under the slide and around the trees. I cannot imagine how she would behave if I didn't keep a leash on her when we go out to walk. The great big world would be one massive distraction that she would not be able to resist, and she would take off in a heartbeat and either be harmed on the roadway, or lost from us forever.

Oh, but how I wish Ava would be like our neighbor's dog. To be able to trust her to stay with me, walk with me, follow my lead. To be able to free her from the leash and know she would not run away—what a feeling that would be for her, and for me. What if God could trust us to walk with Him? What if we could shirk off the leash of limitations and rules and follow God with all of our hearts and be in such good communication with Him that a simple word from His heart to ours would bring us back into step with Him? How freeing would it be to make the choice to walk with God each moment?

God is good, and He knows when we need a leash, and when He can trust us to walk with Him. Let's work to make that spiritual leash come off sooner than later, and enjoy walking by His side and listening to His still, small voice.

Thought-provoker: What spiritual leash do you need to keep you from wandering away from God? What would it take for you to choose to stay by His side and listen to His voice?

Lord, please help me to become a mature, wise child who will stay by Your side and listen to Your voice. Amen.

Notes/Insights:

The Energy Drink

We have a great deal to say about this, and it's difficult to explain, since you have become too lazy to understand. Although by this time you ought to be teachers, you need someone to teach you the basic principles of God's revelation again. You need milk, not solid food. Now everyone who lives on milk is inexperienced with the message about righteousness, because he is an infant.

Hebrews 5:11-13, HCSB

I knew better, but I was being lazy. I wanted a short-cut, an easy way out, so I drank it. It was an energy drink that was supposed to supplement my meal, not replace it. I drank it anyway, and didn't take the time to eat. Then, I went to work out. About an hour in, my muscles got weak; my arms got shaky. I felt a little light-headed. A friend of mine, who is also a P.E. teacher, started asking me about my routine. I told her I had skipped lunch with an energy drink and she chastised me (lovingly, of course.) that they are not meant to replace my food; they were to be used in addition to healthy eating. We left the gym early that day and I got some solid food in my system and felt much better.

How often do we do this in our spiritual lives? Spiritual discipline takes work, and sometimes it's just easier to skip a true meal of feasting on God's Word and settling for a supplement instead. We think listening to praise and worship music will satisfy us. Do not misunderstand, I love praise and worship music, but if that is the only thing sustaining my spiritual walk, I will be wobbly.

Or, perhaps, we substitute traveling prayers for quiet time with God. You know what I mean, "Lord, at least I am talking to You while I am traveling to work, school, etc." We don't give God our undivided attention, and so our spiritual health suffers. We face a trial, or a faith adventure, and we find ourselves weak in our resolve to stand for God, or we find that we are struggling in our faith.

The good news is when we recognize these weaknesses, there is a remedy. Just like finding solid food after my weak day at the gym, when we spend time truly studying and digging into the Word, we find the nourishment we need to restore our souls. When we take the time to pray and truly intercede for others, we find the strength we need to stand (James 5:15-16). We can become mature, experienced believers by taking the time to learn the deep things of God. When we confess our laziness and ask God for renewed determination and wisdom, He grants it (James 1:3-5). There is no reason to be anemic in our spiritual walks. The Word is our meat—we just need to dig in.

Thought-provoker: How strong is your spiritual diet? Are you digesting deep truths from the Word of God? Do you need to confess your laziness and get back into a routine of study and strength?

Lord, You know our spiritual diets; You know where we have become lazy and weak. Help us to strengthen our souls with the meat of Your Word and to enjoy the spiritual feast You have for us. Amen.

Notes/Insights:

More Devotions from Everyday Things

The Olympics

And they sang a new song, saying, "Worthy are you to take the scroll and to open its seals, for you were slain, and by your blood you ransomed people for God from every tribe and language and people and nation, and you have made them a kingdom and priests to our God, and they shall reign on the earth."

Revelation 5:9-10, ESV

Every four years, the torch passes. A new generation takes the spotlight, and the new limits are set. It is not the changing of the political guard; or the presidential elections that capture the world's attention; it's the Olympics. Athletes from all over the world come together to show their skill, talent and training as they compete to stand on the podium as the world's best at their particular sports.

Some of the teams have very definite physical characteristics. God has blessed them with recognizable physical attributes-certain skin pigmentation or facial features that make it easier to determine where they are from. What caught my attention was the diversity of the American team. It seemed that each heritage of American citizenship was represented at the Olympics. Their diversity was so refreshing to me - our land is a place where all are welcome. The prejudice of a few cannot stop the masses from finding a place to call home in America. Peoples from everywhere can come to America and find a way to fulfill their dreams-our athletes did it through hard work and training; with supportive families and friends;

with coaches and staff who helped them stay the course until their hopes brought them to the moment of the Olympics. Someone was crowned victor in each event, national anthems were played, and lifetimes of training and decision were decided.

In Heaven, there will be a Victor crowned-the Lamb, worthy because of the blood He spilled to gain our redemption. He will set up a perfect kingdom, dreams will be fulfilled as we take our places in His divide kingdom after we had accepted His grace of forgiveness (1 Corinthians 3:10-15) and a new anthem will be sung. According to our Scripture passage for today, the new anthem will be the Song of the Lamb-sung by "…every tribe, language, people and nation." People from everywhere can come to salvation through the blood of the Lamb, and on the day He sets up His kingdom, they will be citizens of the land of Eternity. And the glorious moments of the Olympics will pale in comparison to His great light and love for us.

Thought-provoker: Are you a part of the Heavenly citizenship? If you are, praise God for His goodness; if you are not, become one today through the blood of Jesus.

Lord, thank You that You have heavenly citizenship awaiting anyone-no matter their color, language, background or nation. You have blessed us with that citizenship through the blood of Your son, and we are so grateful. Amen.

Notes/Insights:

The Tongue Depressor

～⸺⸺

> For we all stumble in many ways. And if anyone does not stumble in what he says, he is a perfect man, able also to bridle his whole body. If we put bits into the mouths of horses so that they obey us, we guide their whole bodies as well. Look at the ships also: though they are so large and are driven by strong winds, they are guided by a very small rudder wherever the will of the pilot directs. So also the tongue is a small member, yet it boasts of great things.
>
> James 3:2-5, ESV

Well visits. The times scheduled to take the kids to the doctor to be sure they are growing properly, eating right, and growing as they should. We used to call them "check ups." One of the things I noticed the last time we were in for a "check up," was the tongue depressor tumbler. The tongue depressors sit in a clear glass tumbler on the doctor's table. They are clean, rounded pieces of wood that she can use to hold down the tongue so she can get a better look further in. She used the depressor to control the tongue- to keep it out of the way while she was examining the tonsils, throat, etc. The amusing part for me was when she would ask a question, but not move the depressor of the tongue as my child answered. His speech was limited, but he was still able to get his message across.

What if we took God at His Word and allowed His Word to depress our tongues? Our passage today tells us that if we do not stumble in our speech, we can be perfect. But, God sure does know that is impossible for us. That's why His Word must depress our tongues-it needs to make us stop and think before we speak. Do we really need to say that sarcastic comment? Depress it. Do we really need to spurt those angry words? Depress it. Do we really need to make that hurtful sound bite to "get back at that person? Depress it. Can we say something kind? Let that message get out. Can we encourage and build others up? By all means, even as we depress our selfish, sinful words, we can get a message of hope and love across to a lost and dying world. We can be like my son, who answered the doctor's questions, even with the depressor on his tongue. It kept his tongue out of the way as she examined him, just as God's Word can hold our tongue as God examines our hearts and makes sure we are spiritually healthy.

Come to think of it, I think I am going to ask the doctor for a tongue depressor at my next visit, just to remind me to depress those negative words and keep the positive ones coming.

Thought-provoker: How is your tongue depressor working? Are you applying God's Word, the Bible, to your speech?

Lord help us to speak kindness, encouragement, and love into the lives of others and to allow Your Word to depress anything else. Amen.

Notes/Insights:

More Devotions from Everyday Things

Boot Camp for Horses

Consider it a great joy, my brothers, whenever you experience various trials, knowing that the testing of your faith produces endurance. But endurance must do its complete work, so that you may be mature and complete, lacking nothing. Now if any of you lacks wisdom, he should ask God, who gives to all generously and without criticizing, and it will be given to him. But let him ask in faith without doubting.

James 1:2-6, HCSB

"He needs a stronger bit and more exposure."

This was the advice our horse trainer gave us after one day in boot camp. Boot camp for horses is a week, or two, of intense riding/training with an experienced horseman to fix a problem, or to get ready for a new level of competition. Our young horse had sprinted away from the trail and had tried to run through the woods and jump a creek with his rider holding on for dear life. So, the next day, off to boot camp he went.

After just one day, the trainer called with her advice. "A stronger bit will help to control him better, and exposure will help to calm him down. A few more days, and he should be good to take back home." A week later, I led him back into his familiar surroundings. The trainer had ridden him for hours on new trails, exposed him to bull frogs in the creek, birds in the pasture, other horses and loud motorcycles. He was calmer, easier to manage, happier. He had been through the test, and he came through it stronger, wiser and more willing to listen to his master.

We sometimes act like young horses. We get away from the spiritual habits that are good for us, and sometimes, we even drag others along for the wild ride. God, in His infinite wisdom, knows when it is time for a spiritual boot camp. A time when He tests us, breaks us, even puts tough trials on us, so we come through to be wiser, calmer, stronger on the other side. He exposes us to our fears, our worries and our concerns. He shows us His guidance and care are better than those things we fear. He puts the stronger bit of suffering into our lives, not to harm us, but to slow us down and keep us from running through the woods of regret or wallowing in the creek of shame.

The test and suffering do not last forever; we eventually come back to the familiar. But, we are calmer, more trustworthy, and more willing to follow Him, our Master and Lord, and yield to His will for our lives. We become more effective and useful in His plan when we are willing to stay on the path of His will, seek His wisdom, and bend to His hand, so we can enjoy the ride.

Thought-provoker: Are you needing a spiritual boot camp? Or are you yielding to the Master's hand?

Lord, thank You for the opportunity to yield to Your hand and enjoy this ride of life with You in the lead. When I do need to be broken, please use what is necessary to put me back on track with You. Make me willing to grow so I can be calmer and stronger in You. Amen.

Notes/Insights:

The Timing Belt

To everything there is a season, and a time to every purpose under heaven.

Ecclesiastes 3:1, KJV

Thankfully, I was able to pull off the interstate. I was traveling happily on my way to an appointment, when lights on the dashboard suddenly lit up. I looked down to see the lights at the same time that the car started chugging. Yes, chugging. I know that is not a mechanical term, but our mechanic says that females have a certain vocabulary to describe mechanical failures and when men learn to decipher it, it helps them determine what to fix faster.

Anyway, I pulled off the interstate, parked on a side road, and began to investigate. The oil light was on, so I put in a quart of oil. That took care of one problem—only three more lights to go. The check engine light and two others would not go off no matter what I tried, so I called my husband. He told me to bring it home, and then he took it to Tim, our mechanic.

Tim looked it over and found a valve that had clogged, and that clog had allowed the timing to get off in the motor. He is keeping the car for a few days to work on it, flushing the lubrication system, giving it a much needed oil change, and it should be as good as new. A clogged valve knocked off the motor's timing. Much like impatience clogs up the Lord's timing in our lives. That little pressure valve of impatience can cause us to jump ahead of His plans, and cause the whole motor of our Christian life to chug. Or, perhaps it is the valve of procrastination. We know there is something that needs to be done, like an oil change every so many miles for our cars, but we put it off. The valve gets clogged and now the chugging in our lives is due to our lack of determination to do what we know we should do.

How much better if we would simply rest in His perfect timing and allow the motor of life to hum along at His pace? What if we went to God more often and made sure our lives were tuned up and not lacking in the areas of obedience, trust, patience, and courage? Starting today, let us put our lives' timing in the hands of the Master Mechanic, Jesus, and let Him determine what the timing should be.

Thought-provoker: Are you clogging your life's timing with impatience, procrastination or disobedience? Ask the Lord to reveal the clogged valve in your spiritual motor and be willing to take the steps to fix it today.

Lord, thank You that You know all the timing of our lives. Give us the courage to trust You in order for our lives to align with Your will. Help us to be willing to do what You ask, and to wait when You have not revealed what is next. Thank you that Your timing is perfect. Amen.

Notes/Insights:

More Devotions from Everyday Things

Witch's Thistle

And the soldiers twisted a crown of thorns and put it on His head, and they put on Him a purple robe. Then they said, "Hail, King of the Jews." And they struck Him with their hands. Pilate then went out again, and said to them, "Behold, I am bringing Him out to you, that you may know that I find no fault in Him."

John 19:2-4, NKJV

It is no secret that I enjoy gardening. Getting my hands dirty and watching the seeds turn into seedlings, and then grow into full plants that produce fruits and vegetables, is a very rewarding process.

What is very difficult to deal with are the weeds. You see, we had the regular ground-cover type weeds, you pull them out and they keep coming back, but they were not the problem. A pair of gloves and a few minutes each morning, and those types of weeds were manageable. Witch's thistle was the problem. Witch's thistle is a stalk-like plant that grows taller than the vegetable plants, saps much-needed nutrition from the ground, and grows nothing but thorns. Large, pointed, nasty thorns—up and down the entire stalk of the plant. No gloves were thick enough to protect my fingers from those thorns. I tried using a hoe so I would not have to touch them—the stalks slipped through the rungs of the hoe and those weeds stood in defiance of all I tried to rid them from my garden.

My fingers bled from those thorns. The thorns caused inflammation and tenderness in every spot they gouged me. And, I was not intentionally trying to touch those thorns. The thorns Jesus endured for my salvation were pierced into his scalp and head. I have a hard time with the translation of the word "put" in our passage. The Bible is inerrant, and those soldiers did put that crown of thorns on His head—but "put" is such a generic word. These were Roman soldiers, titans of cruelty, who were mocking Him. They "put" that crown on with strength, viciousness and intent to harm. Oh, what Jesus bore for my sin—for your sin! This was just the beginning of His torture as He took on the sins of the world to provide Redemption for all of those who choose to believe He is the Son of God and accept His payment for theirs. He endured beatings, mocking, and yes, the death on the cross. There are no words that adequately express what He suffered, and there are no words that should adequately express our gratitude. We should thank Him with every day of life, and it still will not be enough.

The next time I have to pull out Witch's Thistle, as my finger bleeds, I want Jesus to remind me of the blood He shed for me and thank Him that my thorns are in my garden, and not in my heart.

Thought-provoker: Please take time this Sunday to thank Him, again and again, for all He did for you, and if you have not surrendered to His love—do it today.

Lord, how blessed I am that You took, not only the thorns, but also the entire punishment for my sin. You gave Your life for mine, and there is no way I can ever repay the debt I owe. Thank You for what You did to save me, and please let me never take it for granted. You are so good, and I am so grateful! Amen.

Notes/Insights:

More Devotions from Everyday Things

The Orphan

~~~

There is no fear in love; instead, perfect love drives out fear, because fear involves punishment. So the one who fears has not reached perfection in love.

I John 4:18, HCSB

A young, black and white paint gelding was in the stall when I arrived at the barn one morning. "His owner abandoned him—says he cannot afford him anymore. He's a little hard to handle, but you can work with him if you want to and see what happens." I walked over to the stall and he met me with fear-filled eyes. His ears were up and alert, and his body was tense.

"Easy, fella, I won't hurt you, just want to take a look at you." I tried to rub his forehead, he jerked his head up. I tried to touch his side, he would move away. A halter was out of the question. So, I just sat and talked to him that first day. I spent a week, just talking to him. Then, I went into his stall. Fear welled up in him again, but I just kept talking, moving slowly, and singing. Yes, singing. After a few more days, he would let me touch his side without flinching. We spent one day just getting used to the halter being in the stall. Then, the day came when he finally allowed me to put it over his ears without jerking away. Little by little, "Oreo" came to trust me. We spent time just walking around the pasture—Oreo would just follow me and I made sure nothing would hurt him. Eventually, he trusted enough to let me throw a leg over and sit on him. Then, came the saddle and bridle; the first visit with the farrier, and the first trailer trip. Oreo surprised everyone. I wrapped his legs, put on his halter and lead rope and led him out of the barn to get on the trailer. Everyone was prepared for a fight—trailers are scary places for horses until they get used to them. Oreo watched as I stepped onto the ramp, and without hesitation he followed me right on in. Trust had built a relationship, and that relationship led to no fear. And that was a time for celebration.

God is the relationship Master of this life. He knows how to drive out fear—love. God is love, so He knows exactly how to build trust in us. He keeps all of His promises; He continues to gently speak to us; He won't leave us when fear wells up inside; and He keeps us growing in our love for Him with things He does each day to prove we can depend on Him. I hope and pray that a day comes soon when God leads us into some great adventure—He asks us to trust Him with something scary—and we follow without hesitation. Just like Oreo, we can surprise those around us with our faith, and celebrate with a God like no other.

Thought-provoker: Are you building a relationship with God that is driving out your fear?

Lord, thank You that Your love is the cure for all my fears. I trust You today, knowing You are holy, loving and good. Amen.

Notes/Insights:

The Young Wren

> For this reason, because I have heard of your faith in the Lord Jesus and your love toward all the saints, I do not cease to give thanks for you, remembering you in my prayers, that the God of our Lord Jesus Christ, the Father of glory, may give you a spirit of wisdom and of revelation in the knowledge of him, having the eyes of your hearts enlightened, that you may know what is the hope to which he has called you, what are the riches of his glorious inheritance in the saints, and what is the immeasurable greatness of his power toward us who believe, according to the working of his great might.
>
> Ephesians 1:15-19, ESV

Poor little guy. He didn't mean to get himself trapped, but there he was at 10 p.m., fluttering around in our living room. A young wren, who saw the glowing lights and felt the warmth wisping out our back garage door, was now trapped in our house. He would fly furiously, to the top of the cathedral ceiling, then dive bomb and land on the back of the couch. Then a quick jump to the mantel and a flit to the ceiling fan.

Three of us set a plan to free him. First, we slowly maneuvered around the room and turned off all but one light to lessent his obsession with staying in the room. We opened all the outside doors and turned on the porch lights, and one of us brought the broom in to encourage him to go toward freedom. At first, it looked like he was going for it. He flew toward the front door, but the window above the door distracted him instead and he sound up holding onto the ceiling light chain just inside the door. A ladder and some more coaxing and we thought he would go out, but he flew back into the living room, then the dining room. After several more gentle attempts, we convinced him to fly out the back door and go to freedom. As he did, we cheered.

Sometimes, we are just like that young wren. We have vast freedom in Christ, such a wide sphere to be able to be all He has called us to, but we get distracted by something that confines us. Maybe we made a poor choice in the past and the consequences of the choice have convinced us that we are a house bird, spiritually. We long to fly, but our guilt keeps a ceiling over our heads and every time we go toward freedom the guilt distracts us again. Or, maybe it is the fear of stepping out and doing something "big." God has put the desire in your heart to see Him in a new way - a new faith adventure - but you are like that little bird going around on the ceiling fan. You want to surrender it all, but you don't let loose and soar.

Whatever the reason, God is gently, patiently, urging you to go. Just like us with that young bird, He will encourage you to fly toward freedom. Paul prays for the believers in today's passage to know the hope of God's calling, His glorious riches and His great power among them. Maybe God will use the broom of a message spoken straight to your heart through His Word; maybe He will use the ladder of His glory, so revealed in your life that you cannot ignore His presence; or maybe it will be the consistent, quiet coaxing of His Spirit that will fill you with surrender. Don't wait, or keep fluttering in doubt or fear. Let today be the day you take off and fly for God, and hear Him cheer as you soar.

More Devotions from Everyday Things

Thought-provoker: What is holding you back from soaring? Is it worth it?

Lord, help me to soar for Your glory today and thank You for the freedom I have in You. Amen.

Notes/Insights:

Tammy Chandler

The House Fly

And though the Lord give you the bread of adversity, and the water of affliction, yet shall not thy teachers be removed into a corner any more, but thine eyes shall see thy teachers: And thine ears shall hear a word behind thee, saying, "This is the way, walk ye in it, when ye turn to the right hand, and when ye turn to the left."

Isaiah 30:20-21, KJV

Oh, sweet summertime. The seats get hot, the air is stagnant and the inside of the car is 102 degrees, but there he was; a housefly buzzing around inside the car when we jumped in one morning. We opened all the windows and kept trying to shoo him toward the openings, but he kept bouncing into the windshield. We turned on the fan, we grabbed a loose piece of paper to use as a guide toward the window, we waved our hands, but he still would not go. Four windows opened to the freedom outside that hot, stymie car, but he kept plowing into the windshield, thinking freedom was to be had on the other side of that glass. We gave up, started the car and started on our way to our destination with the housefly buzzing noisily as he head butted the windshield time after time.

How many times have we been just like that fly? God has revealed to us the path to freedom—from a trial, circumstance, or bondage in our lives—but we insist that we know better? We insist that our methods will get us where we want to go, that we can overcome in our own power, and yet we find ourselves head-butting the windshield of defeat. We can see the freedom, but we cannot achieve victory and peace. We refuse to move in the direction that God has directed.

Finally, after several attempts while on the road, my daughter persuaded the housefly that the open window was his true release from the heat of the car. The shooing and the waving finally convinced the little guy the car was not his final destination and he flew off into the morning breeze.

Just like that housefly, we do not belong in the head-butting situations caused by our own pride, stubbornness or conceit. When He sends others to help get us to the window, we need to be willing to accept their guidance and get to a better place sooner. He sends teachers who explain His Word well, and we can trust them to help us find freedom in His principles and precepts. We are to humble ourselves and accept the guidance of our loving God, who wants us out in the breeze of freedom.

Thought-provoker: Are you buzzing like the housefly looking for freedom when God has opened a window for you? Go toward that freedom today.

Lord, thank You for the freedom You give to Your children. Please help us to find Your path and Your way through Your Word and the teachers You have given us. Thank You for freedom and the way to get to it. Amen.

Notes/Insights:

Tammy Chandler

The Dirty Jerseys

If then you were raised with Christ, seek those things which are above, where Christ is, sitting at the right hand of God. Set your mind on things above, not on things on the earth.
Colossians 3:1-2, NKJV

But now you yourselves are to put off all these: anger, wrath, malice, blasphemy, filthy language out of your mouth. Do not lie to one another, since you have put off the old man with his deeds, and have put on the new man who is renewed in knowledge according to the image of Him who created him.
Colossians 3:8-10, NKJV

I like our sons to be active in their sports. I enjoy sitting and watching them play baseball or soccer, as well as joining in on the occasional backyard flag football game. I enjoy watching them progress in their abilities, learn team skills and be a part of something bigger than themselves.

What I do not enjoy is the laundry after those games are played—especially if someone "accidentally" forgets about a smelly jersey in the gym bag or the trunk of the car. It's dirty, yes, but the smell is what really gets to me. I am so grateful for the washer and dryer that take those dirty clothes and make them clean again. The dirt gets washed away and the smell is removed by the detergent as the washer swishes back and forth, and the dryer sheets make the jersey smell pleasant again.

We are supposed to "put off the old man with his deeds." Just like our sons need to strip off those sweaty jerseys and get cleaned up, so we have to do spiritually. And it is not a one-time thing. After every competition, game or scrimmage, those jerseys have to come off and be washed again. It's a daily process when they are in the thick of sport season at our house.

So it is with our spiritual jerseys. We have to keep going to Jesus and asking Him to reveal His image in us. We have to put off those "old man" deeds and put on a new, fresh and clean spiritual jersey—the fruit of the Spirit. We have to "set our minds on things above," and understand the process of sanctification—becoming more and more like Jesus as we walk with Him—involves getting rid of those dirty jerseys and putting on His clean ones. When we are in the thick of the activities of service, we need to make sure our spiritual clothes stay fresh and clean. Salvation took only a moment—sanctification is a life-long process. But don't get discouraged, Jesus has the washing machine of confession and forgiveness, and the dryer of grace and mercy to make sure your spiritual clothes are clean and smell good.

Thought-provoker: Does your spiritual jersey need a washing? Are you putting off the old man and accepting the new man He has for you?

Lord, thank You for clean spiritual jerseys to wear in the fruit of the Spirit. Help us put off the old man and be clean for You. Amen.

Notes/Insights:

Tammy Chandler

Falling Leaves

> For His divine power has given us everything required for life and godliness, through the knowledge of Him who called us by His own glory and goodness. By these He has given us very great and precious promises, so that through them you may share in the divine nature, escaping the corruption that is in the world because of evil desires.
>
> 2 Peter 1:3-4, HCSB

A recent thunderstorm brought some strong winds to our area. The tree in our front yard was whipped and tossed during the storm, and many of its leaves were pulled from their stems. The leaves littered the driveway and stacked against the front steps of the house. They dried out, wilted, and turned brown in a day or two, and our teenage son enjoyed a few moments of "power tool pleasure" as he scattered them into the lawn with a leaf blower.

God's promises are not like those leaves. His Word cannot be stripped from our lives by life's storms, or wilted by heated trials. His promises do not fade or become brittle over time. No, in fact, they become more vibrant and stronger beacons of hope in our darkest moments. God says He has given us everything we require for life and godliness, and His provision is not diminished by our storms and trials. His promises hang tough and hold solid, and we are assured He is faithful.

More Devotions from Everyday Things

So, how do we receive the things we require for life and godliness? "...through the knowledge of Him who called us..." We need to get to know God, the One who stands behind the promises. His very nature gives the promises credibility. He wants us to share in His nature—the promises are rooted in His character. His power is what makes the promises strong and vibrant. Between His character and His power, we have all we need to escape the corruption of this world and its evil desires. Our minds will never be able to comprehend how wonderful He is, but He gives us glimpses of His great character, His divine essence, through the promises He keeps and the power He gives to His children to live. His leaves, His promises, never fall from the tree, and that means we have a lifeline to sustain us through every storm. He is *so* good.

Thought-provoker: Are you clinging to the promises of God's Word in this moment? Do you see beyond the promises to the divine character and unlimited power of your heavenly Father who made those promises? Live today as a child, trusting the Father's word and depending on His power. Take a moment and meditate on how that will affect your life and give you a good day, regardless of what you are facing.

Lord, You are the God behind the promises. You have given me everything, everything, I need to live today in godliness and trust. Fill me with Your presence, and please fill this day with Your power and promises. Help me not to be entangled with the world's nothingness, but filled with Your awesomeness. Amen.

Notes/Insights:

Tammy Chandler

Father's House

> "Let not your hearts be troubled. Believe in God; believe also in me. In my Father's house are many rooms. If it were not so, would I have told you that I go to prepare a place for you? And if I go and prepare a place for you, I will come again and will take you to myself, that where I am you may be also. And you know the way to where I am going." Thomas said to him, "Lord, we do not know where you are going. How can we know the way?" Jesus said to him, "I am the way, and the truth, and the life. No one comes to the Father except through me."
>
> John 14:1-6, ESV

It was a great time. The family got together at our house for a week for the holiday. We had people in every room. Cousins slept on the floor in the kids' rooms. The grandparents were in the extra room; my son slept on the couch so his aunt had a bed. We rearranged furniture so all of us could eat together, and chairs were moved from room to room to play games, do puzzles or watch television. We looked through photo albums, took lots of pictures, and made silly faces. Moments became memories made, and there were lots of hugs and laughter—lots of laughter. Even though we were tripping over suitcases and extra chairs, we were happy to be together.

The last night we were together, I got to thinking about Heaven. No suitcases will be necessary—God will clothe us with perfect clothing, and there will be plenty of room. After all, our Heavenly Father has a mansion full of rooms. And, we will be happy, because we will be together—the great family of God—and He will wipe away every tear. We will spend eternity sharing moments and memories with our awesome Savior and Lord, and with all those who through the ages believed Jesus died for them and accepted His sacrifice in their stead.

Don't be surprised if my earthly family still crowds into one of those rooms, just to be together, and to raise the roof with laughter. Hope to see you there too.

Thought-provoker: Have you become a member of God's family and are you ready for the family reunion of the ages in Heaven? Take a moment to thank God if you are ready to join Him there, and if you are not, accept His offer of sacrifice for you today.

Lord, thank You that we have an eternal, heavenly family reunion coming soon, because You love us so much, and You want us all to be together with You. Amen.

Notes/Insights:

Tammy Chandler

The Remodeling Project

⁘

Therefore, put to death what belongs to your worldly nature: sexual immorality, impurity, lust, evil desire, and greed, which is idolatry... But now you must also put away all the following: anger, wrath, malice, slander, and filthy language from your mouth. Do not lie to one another, since you have put off the old self with its practices and have put on the new self. You are being renewed in knowledge according to the image of your Creator.

Colossians 3:5, 8-10, HCSB

We have been watching friends of ours transform their home. They bought a fixer-upper a year and a half ago, and as they started pulling up flooring and tearing out drywall, they found they had bought more than they bargained for. Black mold from a years-old leak in the drain in the kitchen; mice nests in ceiling light fixtures; floor joists rotted by termite damage—it seemed every room brought its challenges and frustrations. One room at a time, they worked. They pulled out carpet, smashed down walls, and took many, many trips to the dump to get rid of the "old house smell." Sometimes, they asked for help and we had the privilege of going and lending a hand for awhile in their project. Sometimes, they were so exhausted; they just laid down on the couches and rested in the midst of the construction. But, they would get up again and go back to the construction.

And what a transformation. They put in a solid footing under the house to make the floors level, and then they installed beautiful wood floors throughout. The clean, new drywall was a perfect canvas for the beautiful colors they chose for their rooms. They stripped the house all the way to the studs and built back beautiful rooms in the place of the old worn ones. Yes, there were times when they were discouraged, but I also remember the moment when my friend turned and looked at me and said, "I have finally caught the vision, and I love our house."

Oh, that we would get to that point spiritually. After all the work the Master Carpenter, Jesus, is doing in our hearts—tearing out old habits, removing sinful behaviors and replacing them with His character, His love and His teachings. Making our hearts a home fit for the vision He has for us—a beautiful place to dwell with Him while we await our glorious home in heaven. I am so grateful to our friends for allowing us to be a small part of their project, and for allowing us to observe the transformation of their home. My prayer is that we all would catch the vision of what a Godly life looks like and learn to love it, and allow others to help us along the way.

Thought-provoker: Do you love the transformation the Master Carpenter is doing in your heart house? If not, why not?

Lord, thank You for working Your powerful transformation in our hearts. Please help us to love what You are helping us to become and to be happy with holiness today. Amen.

Notes/Insights:

Tammy Chandler

The Tail Wag

> For the Lord himself shall descend from heaven with a shout, with the voice of the archangel, and with the trump of God: and the dead in Christ shall rise first: Then we which are alive and remain shall be caught up together with them in the clouds, to meet the Lord in the air: and so shall we ever be with the Lord. Wherefore comfort one another with these words.
>
> I Thessalonians 4:16-18, KJV

It had been a long day. I had had several appointments, errands, and interruptions, during the day and it was late when I finally trudged through the door. I had an armload of books; grocery bags hanging off both arms, and my keychain was between my teeth so my keys wouldn't get lost. I fumbled with the lock, trying to balance everything as I slipped the key into the lock and turned the handle. I was overloaded and off balance by the time I swung the door open and slid inside. It didn't matter. As soon as she heard the key in the door, she came running. Ava, our puppy, slid around the corner on the hardwood floor, her tail wagging a mile a minute. She kept jumping up so I could see how excited she was to see me.

I plopped my load on the kitchen floor and dropped to my knees; instant puppy kisses on my face and the swish of that tail back and forth. She crawled into my lap, wiggled and wriggled until I had pet every inch of her ears, scratched her belly and rubbed her back. The busyness and frustration of the day melted away as I was engulfed by Ava's greeting. There was no mistaking it—she was thrilled to see me.

I don't think it harms the passage to compare Ava's reaction to my homecoming as to how we will act the day Christ returns. It's been a long time since He's been here, but we know He loves us, and He has promised to return. I know I do not have a tail, but I know my soul will leap with joy at His presence, and I am sure I will show a boat-load of affection for the One who died to save me, and rose again to make me His.

Sometimes, we are too dignified in our thinking. "I would never act like a silly puppy and wiggle into Jesus' lap" we think to ourselves, "how ridiculous." If He lets me, I cannot wait to do just that, and then spend eternity at His feet showing Him my gratitude and love for all He has done. How about you?

Thought-provoker: Are you anticipating Christ's return, or are you too busy to give it any thought? Take some time today to anticipate His return, and thank Him that He is coming.

Lord, thank You for the promise of Your return. May I be so excited that I will not be able to sit still, but show You my praise and affection. Help me to start now, so others will see and become excited too. Amen.

Notes/Insights:

Tammy Chandler

238,000 Miles

≫≪

> For we are laborers together with God: ye are God's husbandry, ye are God's building. According to the grace of God which is given unto me, as a wise masterbuilder, I have laid the foundation, and another buildeth thereon. But let every man take heed how he buildeth thereupon. For other foundation can no man lay than that is laid, which is Jesus Christ. Now if any man build upon this foundation gold, silver, precious stones, wood, hay, stubble; Every man's work shall be made manifest: for the day shall declare it, because it shall be revealed by fire; and the fire shall try every man's work of what sort it is. If any man's work abide which he hath built thereupon, he shall receive a reward.
>
> I Corinthians 3:9-14, KJV

Two hundred and thirty-eight thousand miles—that was all my car had in it. After several years, many road trips, good memories and thousands of errands, it finally died. Thankfully, it quit in the driveway and didn't leave me stranded, but it died, nonetheless.

Two hundred and thirty-eight thousand miles—the lifetime journey of my car. A blessing as it carried me safely where I needed to go and even gave shelter during rain bursts at the soccer field and cold nights on road trips.

So, what is my mileage going to be? How about you? How long will you and I travel on this earth? How far will we go? We do not know; we have no idea if we will live 29,200 days

(80 years), or if our lives will be cut short by an accident, or finished by the rapture. We don't know if our earthly "vehicles" are going to need repairs, will get some dents and dings on the journey, if we will need new set of wheels, or if we will break down. What we do know is every mile matters. People are depending on us—just like I depended on my car. They need us to take them to God, bring them to church, and even provide shelter when life's storms get too harsh and cold.

We need to make every mile count. The passage today tells us it is all watched, stored up, and someday will be tested to see if it withstands. When I think about that car, I remember the times it was trustworthy and safe. We need to be dependable, trustworthy and safe to those who are looking for God in our lives. We need to make sure our life journeys make others want to join us in the direction we are going. We want every bit of our two hundred and thirty-eight thousand miles to matter for Him.

Thought-provoker: Are you making the most of your two hundred and thirty-eight thousand miles? Take a moment to evaluate your journey with the Lord and look for ways to make it matter.

Lord, thank You for the miles You have given us for this life's journey. Help us to make them matter for You. Amen.

Notes/Insights:

Tammy Chandler

The Sewing Machine

> The one who has the bride is the bridegroom. The friend of the bridegroom, who stands and hears him, rejoices greatly at the bridegroom's voice. Therefore this joy of mine is now complete. He must increase, but I must decrease.
>
> John 3:29-30, ESV

I had used it for years. My sewing machine was a gift from my husband our first Christmas after we got married, and I used it for all sorts of projects. I made curtains for our first apartment; birthday presents for family members; clothes for me to wear to work. When the sewing machine finally wore out, my husband replaced it with a newer model. Now, I enjoy using my new machine to work on quilts, sew patches on uniforms and make things our children need. The sewing machine does a great job of stitching seams and making hems. Its job is to do the work, but for its work not to be noticed. After all, do we walk up to someone and say, "That's great stitching on that hem,"? No, we do not pay any attention to the stitches of our clothing—unless they come apart.

Just as the sewing machine's job is not noticed, so are many of the things that we do for the kingdom of God. We are to decrease as He increases. We want Him to receive the glory and the recognition, not ourselves. Barnabas was a great example of going unnoticed. When Saul of Tarsus became Paul of the Gospel, no one wanted to associate him—what if his conversion was not genuine? What if it was a trick? But, "...Barnabas took him and brought him to the disciples." (Acts 9:27). Barnabas took a man who had persecuted the church, consented to the deaths of multiple saints, and he brought him to Jerusalem. He traveled with Paul, and he encouraged him. Several chapters of Acts are dedicated to the journeys of Paul, and Barnabas is right there beside him. He traveled with Paul to Antioch and Iconium. He sailed with him to Cyprus. He saw Paul stoned in Lystra. We do not know a lot about Barnabas, but we know he did the work of a sewing machine. He helped to bring different people together in the kingdom of God, and he did not bring the attention to himself in doing so.

How about us? Are we working to bring people together in the kingdom of God, and not worrying about the attention being upon us? Do we crave the spotlight, or are we steadfast in our good works for the glory of God? When the sewing machine does its job correctly, the one who notices is the seamstress, or the designer. God is the only One who needs to notice what we are doing, and He is the only One who matters.

Thought-provoker: Are you striving to be noticed, or for God to get the glory? Are you willing to encourage others, even if it means you travel alongside?

Lord, thank You for those who encourage others and do not worry about the spotlight for themselves, only You. Help us to be those people today. Amen.

Notes/Insights:

Tammy Chandler

The New Car

But if we walk in the light, as he is in the light, we have fellowship one with another, and the blood of Jesus Christ his Son cleanseth us from all sin. If we say that we have no sin, we deceive ourselves, and the truth is not in us. If we confess our sins, he is faithful and just to forgive us our sins, and to cleanse us from all unrighteousness. If we say that we have not sinned, we make him a liar, and his word is not in us.

I John 1:7-10, KJV

After the car we had driven for so many years finally died, we had to get a new one. It was a very nice car—clean carpets and no marks or dings in the upholstery. We were very grateful for the new car, and we tried very hard to keep it nice and clean. But, baseball practices, trips to the barn, soccer cleats and three different drivers—the car got dirty. There was hay and clay on the floors, and a few wrappers and empty water bottles in the back. What started as a mission to keep the car spotless quickly turned into a battle with real dirt.

So, we pulled out the vacuum cleaner and the trash can. We cleaned all the trash out of the car and then we took turns vacuuming the carpets. We worked hard for a few minutes and the car was back to looking brand new. We wiped down the dashboard, the door handles and the windows, and the car returned to its newly detailed status.

More Devotions from Everyday Things

Our lives are like the new car. At salvation, God gives us a beautifully clean soul. He takes away all our sin, and He gives us a new beginning. But, just like the car, we get dirty. We allow bad attitudes to leave garbage in our hearts; sin leaves its mark on our newly cleaned souls. What are we to do? God tells us to confess our sins to Him, and He is faithful and just to forgive us and cleanse us from all unrighteousness. He does the detail-work to restore our lives and make us look new again. He does the work to wash away the stains and make us clean again.

What if we had ignored the dirt and trash in the new car? It would have continued to build up, to get worse, and become more obvious. The dirt could have marred the carpets as it was ground in by the shoes of multiple drivers. The wrappers and water bottles would have been crushed by back seat riders, and the mess would have become chaotic.

It is the same for our lives—not dealing with our sin will only make it worse. If we say we don't have sin, we deceive ourselves. The mess will be more chaotic the longer we refuse to face it, confess it, and allow Him to cleanse us.

Thought-provoker: Are we confessing our sins daily so they do not pile up and cause chaos in our lives?

Lord, thank You for Your cleansing power. Help us to face our sin and bring it to You, so You can cleanse us. Amen.

Notes/Insights:

Tammy Chandler

The Adventure Continues

༄༅

A man's heart plans his way, but the Lord determines his steps.

Proverbs 16:9, HCSB

Every summer, our family picks an amusement park to attend as part of our vacation. We research what types of roller coasters and rides the park has, what their meal plan is (with three teenagers, that is a must.), if there is a water park, hotels or camp sites close by, and any other facts about the park that will make the day interesting. My husband and the kids love the roller coasters, but I tend to "wander off" while they are experiencing the thrills of being whipped around corners and up and over high hills. I find the swings. Not just any swings—the giant swings. Three hundred feet up in the air, spinning at 50 miles per hour—that is what I enjoy. I can see the entire park from that vantage point, and the wind feels so good on a hot summer day. Each of us enjoys our own type of adventure at the amusement park, and at the end of the day, we are tired, but we have smiles and happy memories of a day spent together as a family.

Life is similar to an amusement park. We make plans, we have dreams, we hope for a good time and sweet memories. We try to find the things in life that challenge us, as well as those things that thrill our hearts and make life worth living. Each of us enjoys something different—some like the wild, crazy thrills of a roller coaster life; others prefer the steady, high in the sky ride like the swings. If we have lived well, at the end of life, we will be tired, but I hope we will each have smiles and happy memories of the adventure we chose to go on with God.

So, find out what your faith-adventure is. Don't worry if it doesn't look like the thrill ride someone else is on; find what makes you trust God, what makes you rely on Him, and what makes your soul feel alive. Live your life so when you reach the end, you will find yourself tired from a good work done for God's glory, you will have a smile, and you will have stored up the memories of a lifetime. Go with God and know He is your Rock, your Hope and your Salvation, and have fun finding Him in the everyday adventures of your life.

Thought-provoker: Are you on a faith-adventure with God, or are you still on the ground wishing to get on the ride of your life?

Lord, thank You for the adventure You have created called faith. As we come to the end of this book, help us to continue to see You in the everyday things, the things that make life worthwhile, challenging, and fun. Help us to see You in every adventure, to join You in the work You are already doing around us, and to know that You are our Hope and eternal Savior. Thank You for the adventure that is just beginning for each of us! Amen.

Notes/Insights:

About the Author

Tammy Chandler is a wife, mother, teacher, friend, author and public speaker. She accepted Christ as Savior when she was five years old, dedicated her life to full-time service as a teenager and has worked in various ministries for the past twenty years. She has a bachelor of education degree from Clearwater Christian College, and a master of education degree from Jones International University. After many years of using everyday objects to teach children and teenagers, God allowed her to write *Devotions from Everyday Things* (Westbow Press) and and its follow-up, **More Devotions from Everyday Things,** to include a larger audience.

When she is not writing, Tammy enjoys spending time with her husband, John, watching their teenage boys play sports, going horseback riding with their daughter or playing fetch with their dog, Ava. The Chandlers live in Tennessee.

Visit Tammy online at:
www.simplydevotions.wordpress.com

Made in the USA
San Bernardino, CA
08 June 2015